THE EVERLASTING GOSPEL

Georg Klein-Nicolai

("Paul Siegvolck")

THE EVERLASTING GOSPEL

*Commanded to be preached by Jesus Christ, Judge of the living
and dead, unto all creatures (Mark 16:15),
concerning The Eternal Redemption found out by sin, whereby
Devil, Sin, Hell and Death shall at last be
abolished, and The Whole Creation Restored to its
primitive purity: Being a testimony against the
present anti-christian world.*

The Everlasting Gospel.

By Georg Klein-Nicolai, 1705.

Originally published as *Das von Jesu Christo dem Richter der Lebendigen und der Todten, aller Creatur zu predigen befohlene ewige Evangelium, von der durch Ihn erfundenen ewigen Erlösung, wodurch alles dem Richter der Lebendigen und der Todten, aller Creatur zu predigen befohlene ewige Evangelium, von der durch Ihn erfundenen ewigen Erlösung, wodurch alles, etc.*

First English edition from 1753.
This edition based on the English edition from 1792.

Front cover illustration by Marcel Rasmussen.

Nylars: Apophasis 2018
www.apophasis.dk

ISBN 978-87-997967-7-9

Das von

JESU CHRISTO

Dem Richter der Lebendigen und der Toden/

Aller Creatur

zu predigen befohlene

Evige

EVANGELIUM

Vn der
Durch Jn erfundenen

Ewigen Erlösung/

Wodurch alles / was da heisset

Teuffel/ Sünd/ Hölle und Tod

endlich gantz und gar vernichtiget/ und also alle Beschöpffe / die von GOtt sehr gut erschaffen worden/
nach gnugsam geoffenbahrter Göttlichen Straff-Gerechtigkeit/ wiederum in ihre urant=
fängliche Reinigkeit und Seligkeit gebracht werden sollen ;

Allen Menschen unter allen Nationen/ und Religions=Parteyen

welche dessen Schall hören/insonderheit abr denen/welche es zu Hertzen nehmen/und sich zu
einer heiligen Gegen=Liebe gegen denso liebreichen GOtt erwecken lassen wollen/

Itzezo

Vor denen nechst=instehenden /a bey denen bereits angegangenen er=
schrecklichen Gerichten über diese gegenwärtige

Wider=Christische Welt/

Entweder zu ihrer Bekehrung und Starckung im dem Guten/ oder Zufalls=Weise zu ihrer Verstockung
und Reiffmachung zum Gerichte; auserbarmender Liebe verkündiget; an unzehlich
vielen Orten durch diesen Druck verbessert/und nebst Hin=
zufügung eines

Neuen Capitels

über Iebr. 2. v. 16.

vom

Namen Abrahä

handend vermehret

von

Georg Paul Siegvolck/

einem einfältigen Schüler der Himmlischen Weißheit.

Gedruckt zu Pamphilia auf Kosten guter Freunde / im Jahr 1705.

Title page of the German edition of Das von Jesu Christo dem Richter der Lebendigen und der Todten, aller Creatur zu predigen befohlene ewige Evangelium, etc. from 1705 published by "Georg Paul Siegvolck".

CONTENTS

PREFACE FOR THIS EDITION

THE EVERLASTING GOSPEL was written by the German pastor Georg Klein-Nicolai (1671-1734) (sometimes spelled Klein-Nikolai) of Friessdorf, and published under the pseudonym "Paul Siegvolck" in 1705. The German title was *Das von Jesu Christo dem Richter der Lebendigen und der Todten, aller Creatur zu predigen befohlene ewige Evangelium, etc.* The English translation was first published by Christopher Sower in Germantown in 1753. It was later published by Elhanan Winchester in London in 1792. It is this edition which is here republished in a slightly updated version.

We do not know much about Georg Klein-Nicolai, but he seems to have been an associate of the radical pietist Johann Wilhelm Petersen and his theology seems to have drawn on Petersen, who was in turn influenced by Jane Leade and the Philadelphians. Johann Wilhelm Petersen was a German-Danish theologian, mystic and pastor at the Lutheran Church in Hanover, and later superintendent in Lübeck and Aue. Johann Wilhelm Petersen grew up in Lübeck where he also studied theology. Together with his wife Johanna Eleonora, he developed a mystic and chiliastic form of pietism in which the belief in Universal Restitution came to play a central role.[1] Georg

---

1   Johann Wilhelm Petersen, *Mystērion Apokatastaseōs Pantōn, Oder Das Geheimniß*

Klein-Nicolai's *The Everlasting Gospel* appeared in the first volume of Petersen's work.[2]

Another source of influence may have been the Schwarzenau Brethren, a radical pietistic group of German Baptists also known as the *Neue Täufer* or the *Tunkers. The Everlasting Gospel* expresses a theological conviction widespread among the Schwarzenau Brethren. Many early Schwarzenau Brethren accepted the doctrine of universal restoration, claiming that after the judgment and punishment described in the New Testament, God's love would eventually restore all souls to God. The leader of the Schwarzenau Brethren, Alexander Mack (1679-1735), seems to have believed that after the collapse of several eternities or *aeons* there would be a final and universal restoration of all things, in which the godless through Christ would finally be saved from their torments in hell.[3]

Mack believed that the punishments described in the New Testament was of temporary duration, but nevertheless of a severe character. But though the doctrine of eternal torment is not supported by scripture, Mack warned that it is much preferable to put one's hope in Christ rather than in the belief that there will be an end to punishments. The belief that God would in the end restore all creation through Christ should not be taken as an excuse for sin. Following Mack, the Brethren often kept their teachings to themselves, and they were largely abandoned by the end of the 19th century. In *The Everlasting Gospel* Georg Klein-Nicolai expressed beliefs simi-

Der Wiederbringung aller Dinge, Durch Jesum Christum (1700).

2   John McClintock & James Strong, *Cyclopedia of Biblical, Theological, and Ecclesiastical Literature*, Volume 10 (1895), pp. 109-33.

3   Alexander Mack, *Rights and Ordinances*; trans. H. R. Holsinger, *History of the Tunkers and the Brethren Church* (Oakland, Cal.: Pacific Press Publishing Co., 1901), pp. 113-115.

lar to that of Mack's. Georg Klein-Nicolai does not, however, seem to have merely accepted soteriological universalism as an esoteric doctrine. Rather, the doctrine was something that was to be widely evangelized, while the teachings opposing the doctrine were considered diabolical.

The belief in a universal reconciliation at the cross leading to a final universal salvation of all, was also present among the Moravian brethren, such as Peter Böhler (1712-1775), who was influential for John Wesley and the Methodist revival in Great Britain and America. Peter Böhler seems to have believed that God would eventually be able to convince all to have faith, thus leading to the final salvation of all. This should remind us that sorts of soteriological universalism akin to that of *The Everlasting Gospel* should not be considered alien or heterodox to the great revivals in the 18th century. It should rather be considered one soteriological view among others. The belief in the final salvation of all need not diminish evangelical fervor and missionary zeal, as is sometimes claimed. Rather, it is exactly because Christ has died to save all, that the gospel must be proclaimed for all.

The arguments put forth in *The Everlasting Gospel* are strongly Biblical and follows the strain of thought recognizable in authors from the Early Church such as Clement of Alexandria, Origen and Gregory of Nyssa, who saw otherwordly torments as temporary and intended for the restitution of the sinner. As such, *The Everlasting Gospel* remains an important and relevant historical witness to the development, influence and reception of the classical Christian doctrine of the restitution of all things (or in Greek *apokatastasis panton*). Even if *The Everlasting Gospel* is not free from errors, and even if the reader cannot follow the author in all of his sometimes extreme conclusions, as when he claims that also the Devil will finally be restored, there are many enlightening passages and useful arguments.

Though many of Klein-Nicolai's claims may seem extreme and unwarranted, his work is a fascinating look into an important part of the history of theological doctrines. Georg Klein-Nicolai seems to have been in no doubt that it is the will of God to restore all fallen creatures. God will attain this purpose, even if the creatures resist him. The belief that creatures are in all eternity capable of resisting God makes creatures stronger than God and thus opens the way to all kinds of "iniquity and atheistic mockery", says Klein-Nicolai. It is only with God's permission that creatures are allowed to resist God. The purpose is, says Klein-Nicolai, that the creatures, who will not voluntarily choose the salvation and well-being offered to them, may taste of the bitter fruits of their disobedience. As a result, the rebellious creatures will finally be conquered and thus give themselves up to their Creator, who is able to subdue all. All punishments are, in the end, redemptive. Though there are minor examples of speculative theology, such as the reasoning that "since God cannot hate himself, he cannot hate his creatures", the conclusions arrived at by Klein-Nicolai are in most instances backed up by biblical references. This is at least true for major claims about the will and capability of God in saving human beings.

Only by introducing speculative elements and beliefs foreign to the Bible does one's conception of God's love become partial and half-hearted. This is not least true for traditional versions of the doctrine of "double outcome", the belief that Jesus Christ will in the end only save a minor part of humankind. In defense of this idea has since the early Middle

Ages been claimed the existence of "two wills" in God, a "hidden God" behind the God revealed in Christ, the existence of a human "free will" making human beings capable of resisting grace, a "double predestination" and so on. Such claims was necessary for explaining why the work of Jesus Christ does only justify and save a few, despite clear scriptural passages such as Rom. 5:18-19. When 1 Tim. 2:3-4 claims that God wants all people to be saved, the traditional argument, repeated by such central protestant figures as Martin Luther, was that God is not bound by his word, and that biblical passages such as these can not be taken at face value, since they are only true of the revealed God.

The author of *The Everlasting Gospel* makes no such speculative claims. Georg Klein-Nicolai's theology is firmly grounded in the biblical belief that God *is* love, and that no created being is capable of resisting the will of God in the end. Rather than introducing foreign elements in his theology Georg Klein-Nicolai shows how seemingly contradictory claims about God's love and willingness to save all on the one hand, and claims about eternal punishment and damnation on the other, can in fact be reconciled on a biblical basis, without making too many speculative metaphysical claims about the nature of God or human beings. The most important argument in the book is perhaps the fact that the biblical concept of "eternity" does in most cases not mean "everlasting" in the sense of endless duration. That the original Hebrew and especially Greek words translated as "eternal" does not mean "endless" and, but "age-enduring", is a well-known fact in scholarship.[4] That most Bible translations still ignore this fact is mostly due to traditionalism.

---

4   Ramelli & Konstan, *Terms for Eternity: Aiônios and Aïdios in Classical and Christian Texts* (Gorgias Press 2007).

Klein-Nicolai saw the doctrine of universal salvation as having a reconciliatory potential between conflicting opinions on the freedom of the human will. As he says, his doctrine shows the right foundation of divine election and eternal reprobation, and demonstrates both to Lutherans and Calvinists as well wherein each party is right, as what they want. Lutheran Orthodoxy is correct in claiming that God wills the salvation of all human beings and that he saves all who in this life come to faith in Christ. Likewise the Calvinists are right in teaching that all who God wills to be saved shall actually be saved. Those whom God will have to be saved, will actually be saved. God plainly declares in his word, that he will have all men to be saved. Therefore all men will be really saved at last. Klein-Nicolai adds that the doctrine of universal restoration is also capable of deciding the dispute with the Roman Catholics about purgatory.

Brought by immigrants across the Atlantic the Everlasting Gospel landed on American soil, where its teachings gained influence as universalism became widespread in the 18th and 19th centuries. This edition includes the original preface to the English edition from 1792 by Elhanan Winchester. Elhanan Winchester (1751-1797) was a Baptist preacher and a co-founder of the United States General Convention of Universalists and the Society of Universal Baptists. Inspired by the teachings of the Everlasting Gospel, Winchester believed that God's love would finally restore everything to its proper place, and argued that the two dominant theological positions of protestantism, Armenianism and Calvinism, in combination lead to the belief that God is both capable and willing of saving all.

This edition has a slightly modernized American English

language, updated formatting and an index of Biblical references. All footnotes have been added by the editor. The text is based on a version from the *Select Theological Library* (1840), digitized by Scot Wells, minister and author of the blog "boyinthebands.com". The original book in German is available on Google Books.

– *Johannes Steenbuch (mercyuponall.org) 2018*

ELHANAN WINCHESTER'S PREFACE

This little book which I now send abroad in this country, was originally written in the German language in the beginning of the present century, and translated into English, and printed in Pennsylvania in the year 1753. I am well acquainted with the good man at whose instance and expense it was translated and printed. He has lived to see the little spark rise into aflame, and the small seed into a large tree, and he may still live many years, until this glorious system, so grand, so worthy of a God, shall have prevailed to bring all the different sects of Christians to be of the same spirit, mind, and judgment.

Then shall the glorious prophecy of Isaiah be fulfilled, "Thy watchmen shall lift up the voice, with the voice together shall they sing; for they shall see eye to eye when the Lord shall bring again Zion."[5] And also that part of our blessed savior's prayer, "That they all (who believe on me) may be one; as thou, Father, art in me, and I in thee, that they also may be one in us; that the world may believe that thou hast sent me. I in them, and thou in me, that they may be made perfect in

---

5   Isa. 52:8

one, and that the world may know that thou hast sent me."[6]

The divisions and animosities among Christians are great hindrances to the conversion of the world to Christianity, and until unity of spirit and harmony of sentiment take place in a much greater degree than at present, we cannot expect the knowledge of the Lord to fill the earth as the waters cover the sea. But that such a glorious event shall take place before the conflagration, is to me as plain as express prophecies can make it, and may the Lord hasten it in his time! The system held out in the following pages appears to me the only one that in the least bids fair to unite the two great bodies of Christians, that have so long and so bitterly opposed each other, viz. those who assert that Christ died for all, and yet that there shall be but few, comparatively, that shall finally derive any saving benefit therefrom; and those who assert that all for whom the savior died shall indeed be saved, but that he died only for a few. For it seems highly improbable that either of these sects should ever so far change their ground, as to go over to the opinions of the other; since one party charges the tenets of the other with want of benevolence, and the other as successfully returns the charge by representing their antagonists as entertaining dishonorable thoughts of the wisdom and power of the Deity. Therefore if a reconciliation takes place between them, it must be on some middle ground where both may meet without giving up their favorite opinions; and this appears to me to be no other but the system of the Universal Restoration; and whenever it shall universally prevail, it will bring this most desirable event to pass.

This book I esteem as valuable on three accounts; First, it was written at a time when this system was but little known,

6   John 17:21-23

having been in a great measure lost during the long night of popish darkness, which overspread the Christian world for so many ages. This little book was at first like a light shining in a dark place, but now the day is broke, and the light shines in a most glorious manner.

Secondly, the author throughout the whole writes like a sincere Christian, appears to have the most glorious ideas of God, of the Lord Jesus Christ, of the divine perfections of the Deity, and of the way of salvation; and he constantly appeals to the sacred Scriptures for the proof of what he writes. And he appears to me as one that had a very serious regard to truth, and to the general welfare of mankind; and while he holds forth the glorious system of the Restoration for the com-fort of the fearful, he speaks in such a manner of the terrors of the Lord, and the punishments of the future state, as is suffi-cient to alarm the consciences of the careless and secure.

Thirdly, it was the first book that ever I saw which treated upon the subject of the Universal Restoration, and it was by reading a little therein, that I first began to turn my thoughts and attention to the system which I now hold forth. Indeed the argument pressed upon my mind in such a manner, that could not get rid of them; and though I strove long against them, yet they conquered me in about three years. I think it was in the year 1778 that I first saw this book, and the first piece I published upon the subject was a sermon delivered April 22nd, 1781, to which I added a list of the passages of the Scripture which I judged to be most in favor of the Restora-tion, and answers to the principal objections most commonly brought against it.

I cannot help therefore having a great regard for this work, as it proved the first mean of my conviction, and at length brought me to embrace this most glorious and universal plan of salvation through Jesus Christ our Lord and savior.

As some of my friends in this country have read, and greatly admired this book, and others who have only seen a part of it quoted in my Lectures have expressed their wishes to have the whole, I have in compliance with their earnest requests, undertaken to republish it, and hope it may be blest to the comfort and salvation of many souls.

I have in some places corrected the language a little, and have made a few small alterations, but in general have followed my author exactly, as he never appears to me to vary from what I judge to be the truth of the gospel.

May the blessing of heaven attend this publication to all who read it, is the earnest desire of one who takes pleasure to subscribe himself a friend to the whole human race.

ELHANAN WINCHESTER.

THE AUTHOR'S PREFACE

Beloved Reader: God, who wills not that anyone perish, but that every one turn to repentance, always used this method, that, before he visited the world, or certain nations, with his judgments, he first poured out upon them all the riches of his long-suffering, love, goodness, and mercy, in such a measure as is allotted to every age; to try thereby, as it were, to his utmost, whether some might be persuaded to forsake their sinful ways, and to be saved from the destruction otherwise waiting for them.

Thus, he gave divers preachers of righteousness to the antediluvian world, and waited full a hundred and twenty years for their repentance. Before God executed the judgment of the Assyrian and Babylonian captivity upon his people of Israel, he did not only first bestow upon them all manner of bodily good, but also sent them many of his faithful servants and prophets, who delivered unto them many excellent prophecies concerning the Restorer of all things, the Lord Messiah. Yea, before he passed the next by far more dreadful judgment upon this nation, he first sent them even his only and most beloved Son, disclosing unto them by him most perfectly his infinite love towards all his creatures; which also afterward he did by his holy apostles.

Now, since verily the future great and terrible day is nigh at hand, wherein the anger of the hitherto so patient LAMB is to be kindled against the present anti-christian world, Rev. 6:16-17, what wonder, then, that God, who willeth not the death of a sinner, is opening at this time all the treasures of his everlasting love towards all his creatures? His design in so doing is, with respect to the wicked, to try his utmost, and to see whether by these means he may bring some of them to repentance, so that they may begin to love again that God who with his eternal love and mercy so tenderly loves them, and thus escape the future terrible judgment, and be able to stand before the Son of man.

But as to the little flock of his faithful, or the bride of Jesus, which is on her pilgrimage in the church militant here on earth, he is leading them now upon Mount Tabor, there to let them see their future transfiguration, yea, the abyss of his perfect love, thereby powerfully to strengthen them against their approaching sufferings, because they will soon be led with their bridegroom, to Mount Golgotha, there to be crucified with him.

For, verily, the perfect deliverance of the children of God will not come till they have been first put to the test in Laodicea, and the empire of darkness has exercised its most extreme fury on them.

Now, for the above-mentioned purpose it is, that this simple testimony of the everlasting and endless love of God towards all his creatures, is recorded in this present little book. If thou, beloved reader, makest proper use of it (to the end whereof I wish thee the necessary light of the Holy Spirit) thou wilt reap abundance of benefit from it in time and eternity, and not know how to thank God, the infinite love, enough for it.

But if thou turnest into lasciviousness, that which is declared unto thee in order to bring thee to repentance and true amendment of life, and if thou dost pervert it to fortify thyself in thy carnal security; then will, O man, thy doom be just in the day of judgment, nay, even in this world, may thy outward state and condition here be whatsoever it will, emperor, king, prince, count, baron, gentleman, citizen or peasant, rich or poor, learned or unlearned. I and all the children of love, who by the enlivening knowledge of the everlasting love of God, which is represented unto thee in this treatise, quite plain, and without obscure enigmatic or proverbial sayings; we, I say, who are not made careless by such love of God, but daily more and more sanctified and mightily encouraged for our spiritual combat against the devil, world, sin, hell, and death, we will assist in condemning thee. Yea, this little book, which now is given thee as a mean of life, shall then become thy death, a worm which will gnaw thee day and night, an inextinguishable fire. The Lord preserve thee from it, if thou desirest to be preserved.

If anyone should undertake rashly to contradict the eternal truth set forth in this treatise, or to write against it, he may do it at his peril; but then I would have him to know, that the empty vapors of the glosses of his reason will never be able to obscure the bright sun-beams of so many clear testimonies of the Holy Scripture, which treat of the everlasting love of God towards all his creatures; (especially as they are exhibited in the 12th chapter of this treatise) and that I count him too feeble and unable to thrust that God from his throne, who is everlasting love towards all his creatures, and to enthrone a strange God, who is to be worshiped as endless fury towards most of his creatures.

And if anybody shall go so far as to calumniate this testimony of eternal truth, and to persecute my person, as much as lies in his power, he must know, that I will not be revenged on him in any other way, than by offering him up day and night to the endless and tender love of God, together with all the rest of corrupt creatures, being prisoners in the center of wrath, to the end that they may every one of them, by Christ Jesus, the Son of eternal love, be brought back again into the center of eternal love, whence they are fallen, and thus enjoy for ever and ever, that God who is nothing else but love! Yea, Amen, so be it, Lord Jesus, thou eternal and universal savior, Amen!

THE EVERLASTING GOSPEL

By Georg Klein-Nicolai ("Paul Siegvolck")

"Then I saw another angel flying directly overhead, with an eternal gospel to proclaim to those who dwell on earth, to every nation and tribe and language and people."
(Rev. 14:6)

I.

GOD, IN HIS WORD, DESCRIBES HIMSELF AS THE EVERLASTING, ESSENTIAL LOVE; AND THE RESULT THEREOF.

NONE can better describe God, than God himself, or the Holy Spirit of God which testifies of him in the sacred Scriptures.

> *"No man hath seen God at any time: the only begotten Son, which is the bosom of the Father, he hath declared him."[7] (John 1:18)*

> *"The Spirit searcheth all things, yea, the deep things of God. For what man knoweth the things of man, save the spirit of man which is in him? Even so the things of God knoweth no man, but the Spirit of God."[8] (1 Cor. 2:10-11)*

The Holy Spirit describes God, or the Divine Being, thus, that he is a spirit;[9] a consuming fire;[10] light, without darkness.[11]

> *"The Father of Lights, from whom every good gift, and every perfect gift cometh down, with whom is no variableness, neither shadow of turning."[12] (James 1:17)*

But all descriptions of the Divine Being, that we find in the

---

7   John 1:18
8   1 Cor. 2:10-11
9   John 4:24
10 Heb. 12:29; Deut. 4:24
11 1 John 1:5
12 James 1:17

Holy Scriptures, together with all that may be believed, thought, or uttered of God, center in this one word, Love; which the Spirit of truth attests by John, saying:

> *"He that loveth not, knoweth not God; for God is Love.*
> *And we have known and believed the love that God*
> *hath to us. God is Love, and he that dwelleth in love,*
> *dwelleth in God, and God in him."*[13] *(1 John 4:8-16)*

If God is Love essentially, and so that God and Love is one and the same thing, it undeniably follows, that whatsoever God doth (though in our eyes it should appear to be the most terrible affair) proceeds from Love, because God, who does it, is Love itself: as, on the contrary, whatsoever Satan doth, let it appear never so good and useful, proceeds from hatred against God and his creatures.

All works, that are not works of love, in their very principle, or spring from it as their center, are not the works of God; because God, as the essential, everlasting, unchangeable love, can do no other but works of love. As the tree is, so are its fruits.[14]

All creatures, considered in themselves, without their coherent corruption, are productions of the eternal love of God.

> *"For of him, and through him, and to him, are all*
> *things."*[15] *(Rom. 11:36)*

> *"Thou art worthy, O Lord, to receive glory, and honor,*
> *and power: for thou hast created all things, and for*
> *thy pleasure they are, and were created."*[16] *(Rev. 4:11)*

Therefore, since God cannot hate himself, he cannot hate his

---

13 1 John 4:8–16
14 Matt. 7:16–18
15 Rom. 11:36
16 Rev. 4:11

creatures, or that in them which his hands have made.

> *"For thou lovest all the things that are, and abhorrest*
> *nothing which thou hast made; for never wouldst thou*
> *have made anything if thou hadst hated it."[17] (Wis.*
> *11:20)*

So that whatsoever God, who is Love, doth and purposeth
with his creatures, as noble productions of his love, both in this
and in the future ages, must proceed from love, and thus with respect to the creatures, all the purposes of God must have something good and salutary for their ultimate end.

> *"For the Lord will not cast off forever. But though he*
> *cause grief, yet will he have compassion according to*
> *the multitude of his mercies. For he doth not afflict*
> *willingly, nor grieve the children of men."[18] (Lam.*
> *3:31-33)*

Now, as it is the love of God that made the creatures, that
through Christ redeemeth them from sin and the curse, that
sanctifieth and purgeth them from all disorder, that protects and
preserves them, and bestows all manner of good upon them;
even so it is the same love which punisheth the creatures when
they are found in rebellion against their Maker, and do not continue in the order in which he first created them.

> *"As many as I love I rebuke and chasten: be zealous*
> *therefore and repent."[19] (Rev. 3:19)*

Hence, all punishments wherewith God visits his creatures, as
far as they come from him, and are considered according to their
first principle, are works of divine love.

---

17 Wis. 11:20
18 Lam. 3:31–33
19 Rev. 3:19

If all punishments determined by God for the creatures, be they never so dreadful, are (when considered according to their inmost center and principle) works of divine love, it necessarily follows from hence, that even the most dreadful punishments which God, in the age or ages to come, will inflict on bad angels and men, as far as they proceed from him, are grounded on no other principle than that of love; since God, who condemneth and sentenceth the corrupt creatures to such punishments, is the essential, everlasting, and unchangeable love, and nothing else but pure love, and will remain such unto all endless eternities, and therefore, all, whatsoever comes from him, must proceed from love. If such punishments, on God's side, had any other ground but love, then would that God, who punisheth his creatures from such a ground, be no God; because the true and only God, besides whom none other is to be found, is nothing else but pure love, and who therefore can do nothing else but what springs from the center of love, and returns into the same.

> *"Thus saith the Lord, the King of Israel, and his*
> *Redeemer the Lord of Hosts, I am the first, and I am*
> *the last, and besides me there is no God."*[20] *(Isa. 44:6)*

And this God, besides whom there is no other, is love.[21]

Hence, it follows, without contradiction, that not one of those punishments which God has determined for the depraved creatures can be intended for the never-ceasing, and endless perdition and torment of those intelligences that had their origin from the unchangeable love of God; but they must aim at, and be designed for, their final preservation, melioration, and restoration, let them last as long as they will; because the deepest ground of all punishments determined by God, for the creatures, so far as they are his doing, is his infinite and unchangeable love. And it

---

20   Isa. 44:6
21   1 John 4:8; 1 John 4:16

is impossible that love should, without end, plague and torment that which it loves; but by all pains and torments, seeks, and can seek, nothing else but the amendment of its beloved object. For love thinketh no evil;[22] much less does evil, or designs to do it.

---

22   1 Cor. 8:5

II.

WHAT THE WRATH OF GOD IS, AND HIS JUSTICE IN PUNISHING.

AS the whole Divine Being is pure love, so are likewise all the attributes of God; as for instance, his wisdom, omnipotence, holiness, mercy, truth, etc. at the bottom nothing else but love. If anything could be said of God, which is not grounded upon love, or is contrary to it, God would have something in himself, which would make him to be no God, because the true and only God is entirely an ocean of love.

From hence may be easily conceived what God's wrath is, and his justice in punishing, of which the Holy Scriptures, both in the Old and New Testament, make mention so frequently; namely, such wrath and punishing justice of God, is, as all other divine attributes, nothing else but his essential love, which, as it shows itself pure with the pure,[23] that is, deals most kindly, lovingly, and bountifully with those creatures who stand in their right order, in true humility, and subjection to God; so with the froward it will show itself froward, or unsavory.[24] That is, with the perverse, rebellious, and proud creatures, who do not stand in that true order wherein God would have them, but are disobedient, and will not be subject unto him; with such it will deal hardly, and, as it were, act perversely with them: "for God resisteth the proud,"[25] and he will torment them by all manner of bodily and spiritual plagues, both in this, and the next age, until they shall be subdued, and shall acknowledge their offenses,

---

23   2 Sam. 22:26-27
24   Psalm 18:25-26
25   1 Pet. 5:5

humbling themselves with their whole heart, before the righteous God, and in so doing shall be made partakers of the sweet effluence of his infinite and everlasting mercy and love.

So God is terrible, both in this and the other world, for this end only, that at the last he may be gracious and merciful to those to whom he has been terrible. In short, God, when he is angry, doth a strange work, both in this and the next age, to the end that afterward he may do his proper works, which are those of love, grace and mercy.

> "For I will not contend forever, neither will I be always wroth, for the spirit should fail before me, and the souls which I have made."[26] (Isa. 57:16)

> "He will not always chide; neither will he keep his anger forever."[27] (Psalm 103:9)

> "For God hath concluded them all in unbelief, that he might have mercy upon all."[28] (Rom. 11:32)

God always continues the same towards all his creatures, and his nature, which is love, is unchangeable, therefore all the anger of God, both in this world and that which is to come, hath only love for the foundation of its working; yea, it is in reality nothing else but his essential and ever abiding love, which must compel those creatures by terrible judgments to obey him, that will not be brought to it by fair and gentle means; nevertheless so, that the obedience to which they are brought in such a dreadful manner, doth not remain forced; which is to be concluded from this, that the whole creation shall at last praise God.[29] And the

---

26 Isa. 57:16

27 Psalm 103:9

28 Rom. 11:32. See also Deut. 28:15-68 compared with Deut. 3:2–6, etc. compared with Lev. 26:14–45

29 See Rev. 5:13 compared with Psalm 150:6

reason for it will indisputably be, because that all shall taste and see that the Lord is good, and that it is well with those that obey him.[30]

Hence, it clearly appears, that it is impossible, that the wrath of God, and his justice in punishing (since they have nothing else but the essential love of God, for their deepest principle), should be designed for, and tend towards the endless perdition of those creatures that were produced from God's everlasting love, and which God, as such, can no more hate than he can hate himself; but that God in all these punishments, can have no other final view than the rooting out of sin, and the mending and restoration of the corrupt creatures.

And in such a sense it is that God is called in the Holy Scriptures a consuming fire, not as if he intended entirely to consume his creatures, or to plague and torment them without end; but because he will consume the evil in and about his creatures, which by their willful turning away from God, they have brought upon themselves, and mixed with their being, and which he will at last extirpate out of his whole creation, and every individual creature, and annihilate it; which certainly cannot be done without great pain to the corrupt creatures, whose whole will is so coherent with evil. The whole creation "shall be delivered from the bondage of corruption into the glorious liberty of the children of God."[31]

> "Then shall be brought to pass the saying, that is written, death is swallowed up in victory. O death, where is thy sting! O grave, or hell, where is thy victory? The sting of death is sin."[32] (1 Cor. 15:54-56)

---

30 Psalm 34:8
31 Rom. 8:21
32 1 Cor. 15:54–56

"Death the last enemy shall be destroyed."[33] (1 Cor. 15:26)

"Behold the Lamb of God who taketh away the sin of the world"[34], where I would have you consider in the original, the force of the expression "sin of the world", and the word "take or bear away", which properly signifies, to make that something which now exists, to be hereafter no more. Such a savior and Redeemer we have in the person of Christ, who will take away the sin of the world; that is, he will by the power of his most precious blood, shed for the sins of the whole world, bring things at last to such a pass, that no sin at all, and consequently, not the least evil will anymore be found in the world, or in the creatures of God, but be totally destroyed and swallowed up in victory, together with the wages of the first and second death, depending thereon.

---

33   1 Cor. 15:26
34   John 1:29

III.

EVERY THING THAT GOD WILLETH, MUST ABSOLUTELY BE FULFILLED AT LAST; AND WHAT IS TO BE CONCLUDED THEREFROM.

EVERY divine will, let it be conditional or absolute, is in great earnest, and of almighty power, and must therefore infallibly and actually be fulfilled at one time or another, be it never so long delayed.

> *"Whatsoever the Lord pleaseth, that did he in heaven, and in earth, and in the seas, and all deep places."*[35] *(Psalm 135:6)*

> *"And he doeth according to his will in the army of heaven, and among the inhabitants of the earth: and none can stay his hand, or say unto him, what doest thou?"*[36] *(Dan. 4:35)*

He "worketh all things after the counsel of his own will."[37]

Now since God in his word so earnestly declares, and hath confirmed the same by a most solemn oath, that he hath "no pleasure in the death of him that dieth, nor in the death of the wicked; but that the wicked turn from his way and live."[38] That he is "not willing that any should perish, but that all should come to repentance."[39] That he "will have all men to be saved, or restored, and to come unto the knowledge of the truth."[40] That at

---

35   Psalm 135:6
36   Dan. 4:35
37   Eph. 1:11
38   Ezek. 18:23; Ezek. 18:32; Ezek. 33:11
39   2 Pet. 3:9
40   1 Tim. 2:4

last he will make all things new, nothing excepted.[41]

It unavoidably follows, that his divine will must be finally accomplished in respect to all, and every one of his creatures, whose death and destruction he willeth not, whom he will have to be saved, and which he will make new. If it be not done in the present time, as indeed it is not but to the smallest number of the corrupt creatures, it must necessarily be done in the age to come, at least before that period when Christ, after all things shall be subdued to him, and subordinate under him, that is, restored to that true order, in which they were created by him in the beginning, shall deliver up the kingdom to the Father, even the whole restored creation; to the end that the most Holy God, who cannot unite himself with anything that is impure, may be all in all, and fill all with his glory.[42]

The Holy Scripture declares that wicked men both can and do oppose and resist God;[43] As also that no creature can resist the will of God.[44] Though here seems an apparent contradiction, yet both these positions may well consist together; and here may be said, distinguish between the times, and the Scriptures will agree.

The creatures may withstand the will of their Creator; but this is not to be understood in such a manner, as if there was an ability and power in them, whereby they might as it were, repel and conquer the power and might of God that works in and upon them, so that the same could never get its last end with such rebellious creatures. For it is only with God's permission, and as long as he thinks fit that the creature is suffered to withstand or resist God, for reasons best known to him, and to the end that the creatures, who will not voluntarily choose the salva-

---

41 Rev. 21:5

42 See 1 Cor. 15:24–28; Col. 1:16 compared with Gen. 1:81

43 Matt. 23:37; Matt 22:3; John 5:40; Acts 7:51

44 Rom. 9:19; Dan. 4:35

tion and well-being offered to them, may taste of the bitter fruits of their disobedience, and on themselves learn to know the difference between good and evil, which before they would not believe, when God in his word did set it before their eyes; which, through the wisdom and mercy of God, will at last have this good effect upon the malicious creatures, that they will, as conquered, give themselves up to their Creator, justify the punishment of their transgressions, and praise the most holy justice of God manifested therein, and consequently humble themselves before the Supreme Being, who is able to subdue all, however great, mighty, haughty or malicious they may be; and thus by the grace of God, which they will embrace anew after they have suffered their punishment, they shall be divested of all their obstinacy.

Of this only true and certain way for the restoration of all stubborn and rebellious creatures, God has showed us a very remarkable instance in Nebuchadnezzar, as a pattern of the rest of obdurate men and creatures. The confession of this haughty monarch, concerning the most High King of Heaven, after he had felt the weight of his punishing hand, will ever hold true.

> *"He doeth according to his will in the army of*
> *Heaven, and among the inhabitants of the earth: and*
> *none can stay his hand, or say unto him, What doest*
> *thou? All his works are truth, and his ways judgment,*
> *and those that walk in pride he is able to abase."*[45]
> *(Dan. 4:35-37)*

It is therefore clear, that no creature can resist the Creator to all endless eternity, or as long as God is to remain God, but only to a certain period or age, be that short or long, 10, 100, 1000, 10,000, 20,000, 40,000 or more years, yet at last it must come to

---

45   Dan. 4:35-37

an end.

For if it was possible for the creatures to resist their Creator in such a manner as to repel and conquer his Almighty and Divine power, by the power of their iniquity, and consequently without God's permission and the withdrawing of his might, to withstand him, and to continue in obstinacy, bitterness, hatred and enmity against him, and what is more, to all endless eternity, and as long as God shall exist (as has been commonly taught) it would indisputably follow, that the creature, and that which is evil, is as strong, or stronger than God, and that which is good; or that the will of God is not in earnest, when he with so many solemn expressions declares, that he heartily desires the salvation of all men; that he is not pleased with the destruction, death, and misery of his creatures; but rather earnestly requires, that they should repent and live; and that he will make all things new. But neither can be thought of God without the greatest blasphemy, as it would entirely overthrow the whole Divine Being, make God to be no God, but an impotent idol, or a hypocrite; and consequently quite open the way to all iniquity and atheistic mockery.

IV.

IT IS IMPOSSIBLE THAT TWO CONTRARY THINGS SHOULD BE BOTH OF ENDLESS DURATION.

IT is as impossible that there should be two endless contrary things, as that there should be two real contrary Deities, a good God, and a bad one, or two sorts of contrary creatures, both of truly divine origin, some being made good by God, and others bad.

For an absolute and merely infinite duration, which has neither beginning nor end, is, according to the confession of all divines, yea, of every reasonable man, a property peculiar to the uncreated Being only. But such an infinite duration, which although it has a beginning, yet shall have no end, can only be the property of those creatures that are of divine original. For as these, according to the language of Scripture, are of divine origin, and therefore are rooted in God, or in his almighty creating power, which has no beginning, they can also be everlasting, their existence or duration can also be without end in God.

"For in him we live, and move, and have our being.
For we are also his offspring."[46] *(Acts 17:28)*

But whatsoever has not its eternal root in God, or in his eternal creating power, but is sprung up in the creature in this world, by its voluntary turning away from God, and against his holy will, and consequently is an abomination and displeasure to the Most High, and is only suffered by him, such as sin, and the punishment depending thereon, these things cannot possibly be of an absolutely endless existence, and duration, or remain so long

46 Acts 17:28

41

as God shall exist; but must of necessity cease at last, and be annihilated.

For as God is a Being to those creatures which he created good, and which exist through his will, whereby they may subsist and be preserved without end; so he is, on the contrary, to iniquity and sin (which against his will is sprung up in and sticks to the creatures) a consuming fire, whereby all sin and perverseness in the creatures must be at last consumed, annihilated and separated from them in the highest degree, in order to restore them to their primitive purity; in the same manner as fire does not consume and destroy the gold, but only the dross and that which is impure.

Now all those who pretend that the degeneracy and sin found in fallen angels and men, together with the punishment following it, are of an absolutely endless existence, and will continue so long as God exists, make sin either a God, or a creature of divine original; but how much this resembles the heresy imputed to the Manicheans, is left to their own judgment; or they deny that God is entirely a consuming fire to sin, because, according to their pretense, he either cannot or will not destroy it in most of the creatures; and consequently represent him either an impotent God, or one who takes delight in sin and the punishment of it. For what man will suffer that continually before his eyes which is loathsome, or an abomination to him, if he has it in his power to remove it? Since God, therefore, has so earnestly declared in his word, that all sin is an abomination unto him, and that he takes no pleasure in the punishment of it; yea, that his end, in sending his Son, is utterly to destroy sin and death, and essentially to restore an eternal righteousness to all mankind, who all both sinned and died in Adam; so that "As by the offense of one, judgment came upon all men to condemnation; even so by the righteousness of one, the free gift came upon all men, onto justification of life."[47] It is evident, that all those who by their tenets maintain, that God will suffer sin and the punishment of death in and upon his creatures to all endless eternity, which by his almighty power he can destroy, and hath solemnly promised that he will destroy, make the most true and holy God a liar and a hypocrite, and contrary to his own plain words accuse him of taking delight and pleasure in sin, and the punishment of death depending thereon.

---

47   Rom. 5:18

V.

THE DIABOLICAL NATURE, AND THAT WHICH MAKES FALLEN ANGELS TO BE DEVILS, MUST BE WELL DISTINGUISHED FROM THEIR ANGELICAL NATURE IN WHICH THEY WERE CREATED; AND THE RESULT THEREOF.

Two things are to be considered in all fallen and corrupted creatures. First, that nature in which God created them in the beginning; and, secondly, the degeneracy and sin, which through the creature's own fault has intermixed with that nature.

For instance, the soul and body, with all their powers and faculties, viz. the faculty to understand, to will or desire, to love, to act, to see, to hear, to smell, to feel, to taste, etc., may be truly called the nature of man, in which God created him. But what is called sin, vice and degeneracy, and which coheres, and is intermixed with, the human nature, since the fall, is this, that man's understanding is darkened; his will, desires, and affections, are not fixed upon God and everlasting things, but upon the creatures, and those things, which are transitory and vain; and that man, according to his perverse will and desires, and the blindness of his mind and understanding, does not apply the rest of the faculties of his soul, and his body with all its limbs, to that use which is agreeable to God, but, on the contrary, to such things as displease him. Sin, therefore, consists in nothing else but disorder and abuse; and when a man is converted, and of a sinner is made a godly and holy man, he goes over from the disorder and abuse of his nature, to the true order and right use of it. Paul thus expressed the difference:

*"As ye have yielded your members servants to
uncleanness and to iniquity, even so now yield your
members servants to righteousness unto holiness."[48]
(Rom. 6:19)*

*"I beseech you, brethren, by the mercies of God, that
ye present your bodies a living sacrifice, holy,
acceptable unto God, which is your reasonable
service."[49] (Rom. 12:1)*

Now, as sin, which cleaves to the depraved creatures, is the only thing which God hates, so it appears impossible for him to hate in itself the being or nature of his creatures, let them be never so corrupt; but as he loved them when he created them, he will love them to all endless eternity, because, as creatures, they are the productions of his eternal, unchangeable love.

*"For of him, and through him, and to him are all
things."[50] (Rom. 11:36)*

*"Thou art worthy, O Lord, to receive glory, honor, and
power: for thou hast created all things, and for thy
pleasure they are, and were created."[51] (Rev. 4:11)*

*"For thou lovest all the things that are, and abhorrest
nothing which thou hast made: for never wouldst thou
have made anything if thou hadst hated it."[52] (Wis.
11:24)*

Although creatures that are endued by God with a free will,

---

48 Rom. 6:19
49 Rom. 12:1
50 Rom. 11:36
51 Rev. 4:11
52 Wis. 11:24

may spoil themselves through the abuse of that free will, yet no creature of itself can annihilate that being or nature which God gave it, or make something so quite different of it, that nothing of a creature of God shall remain. For as no creature can give itself a being, so neither can it take away or annihilate its own being. And as it is only the Omnipotence of God which is able to produce conscious intelligent beings, so also nothing less than the same almighty power is able to take away the existence of those creatures which he hath made. As long, therefore, as a creature remains a creature, so long something remains in it which God truly loves, viz. that being which he gave it; suppose the same to be never so disordered and corrupt.

Now all this is to be well considered with respect to fallen angles: for then we shall be able to discern the deepest ground for the mystery of their restoration, and consequently comprehend it the more easily.

I mean, we must learn well to distinguish between that angelical nature in which God created them, and the iniquity and sin, which, through their own fault, has intermixed with such nature, the source whereof is their perverse self-will, that caused them to leave their center and principle of humility (wherein alone a creature can be happy) and to withdraw themselves from their obedience and subjection to God, and to rely on themselves, willing to live independent of God, nay indeed, to be themselves God. For each an independence as admits of none superior, or where one needs not to be ruled by the will and command of another, is, and always must be an essential property of the great God and Creator of all things, and cannot by any means belong to a creature, nor can be ceded to it by God, who will not give his glory to another.[53]

Therefore the Scripture very emphatically says of the devil,

---

53   Isa. 42:8; Isa. 48:11

that he abode not in the truth.[54] And that the angels kept not their first estate, but left their own habitation.[55]

Now this perverse self-will in the fallen angels, together with all the iniquity that is in it, and produced thereby, is the proper diabolical nature, or that which makes them devils and enemies of God; and this alone is the thing which is an abomination to him, and what he hates in them.

But that an angelical nature in itself, in which God first created the fallen angels, and to which the iniquity, degeneracy, and perverseness so closely cleave, or rather have quite penetrated through, and intermixed with, that I say is no devil, but according to the confession of all reasonable men, a good creature of God, a production of eternal love, which the Creator as truly loves, as he loves the being and nature of men, yea, as himself, and will love to all endless eternity; and consequently, by virtue of such his everlasting, unchangeable, and almighty love, will of necessity bring it once into the right order again. For, as by Christ he has created all things that are in heaven and that are in earth, visible and invisible, etc.[56] (to which likewise indisputably belongs to all fallen angles) even so it has also been the good pleasure of God to reconcile all those things (which were created by Christ) unto himself, whether they be things in earth, or things in heaven;[57] that is, by the power of his blood, shed for the sins of all, to make them fit and capable of being restored from their disorder to their first right and true order, though every one in his own time, so that at last not only the wrath of God may be turned away from the creatures, but also the enmity of the creatures themselves, cease, and the sorrow which the good and holy creatures of God really feel for their fallen and corrupt

54 John 8:44
55 Jude 6
56 Col. 1:16
57 Col. 1:20

fellow creatures, may be no more; but universal joy, and everlasting praises to God may be caused and raised in the whole creation. The words of God, that he will make all things new,[58] are true, whether men believe them or not: their unbelief will not make the promise void. For as every thing was very good when first created by God, for God saw every thing that he had made, and behold it was very good.[59] So when he shall make all things new, there will be neither sin, death, nor hell, nor sorrow, crying, nor pain, throughout the whole creation, which shall then be wholly delivered from the bondage of corruption, into the glorious liberty of the children of God.[60]

All men who rashly dare exclude one of the fallen creatures, be it never so corrupt, from the endless mercy and all renewing love of God, are not yet grounded in that love to enemies, which is so highly recommended to us by the universal savior of the world,[61] which distinguishes true Christians from unbelievers and is the surest sign of our being the children of God. They are not grounded in humility, because they have not that deep sense of their own misery and most abominable condition by nature, that they ought to have; and consequently cannot duly pity other corrupt creatures as they ought, considering them as God's creatures.

They are respecters of persons, and so not altogether made partakers of the divine nature; since with God, who is everlasting love towards all his creatures, as such, no respect of persons finds place.[62] They do not yet know what that Scripture meaneth, "For God hath concluded them all in unbelief, that he might have mercy upon all"[63]; And indeed God's mercy is not only towards

---

58   Rev. 21:5
59   Gen. 1:31
60   Rom. 8:21
61   See Matt. 5:44–48; Luke 6:27–36
62   Acts 10:34; Rom. 2:11; Col. 3:25
63   Rom. 11:32

all men, but also according to the plain testimony of truth, over all his works;[64] to which indisputably the fallen angels belong, who in the beginning were even some of the most glorious and chief works of God, the Holy Spirit in the Scriptures calling them principalities, powers, and rulers.[65]

Those men do not understand how necessary that knowledge is, which Paul wishes all believers to "be able to comprehend with all saints, what is the breadth, and length, and depth and height, and to know the love of Christ, which passeth knowledge" (or as the original may signify, to know that the love of Christ far supasseth all knowledge), that they might be filled with all the fulness of God, in such a manner as to see that it extends over the whole creation, and every individual creature.[66]

From which it follows, that those cannot be filled with all the fulness of God, who will not comprehend with all saints what is the breadth, and length, and depth, and height of the love of God, and that it is broader, longer, deeper, and higher, than all sin which is to be found in the creatures, with the corruption depending thereon; yea, who will not know, that the love of Christ infinitely surpasseth all knowledge of men and angels, but dare presumptuously confine it within the narrow limits of their own knowledge, and tenets taught by corrupt human reason. In short, these men who murmur against the goodness of the heavenly Father of the family, and complain of his everlasting love and mercy, may find both their pictures drawn, and their lessons

---

64 Psalm 114:9
65 Eph. 6:12
66 Eph. 3:18-19

given them, in Matt. 22:10–16[67], and Luke 15:28–32[68].

Now if that man, who, regardless of all remonstrances, would audaciously exclude but one creature from the endless mercy of God, deserves such a censure, what shall we say of those, who with great assurance, dare exclude from it so many thousands of millions of creatures, that through the blood of Christ are all made fit for redemption and reconciliation? Ah! May these poor men be prevailed upon, by the wounds of Jesus Christ, the universal savior of the world, and by the everlasting mercy and love of God, which will most tenderly embrace them too, to pity, in this case, their own souls, and to consider what an abominable arrogance it is, to make the love of God, which has no limits, much less than the love of men, who are bound to love even their worst enemies, and to recompense all evil with nothing but good; and yet with all their love they are no more to be compared with God, and his love, and mercy, than the least worm that creeps on the ground, and is trodden under foot, is to be compared to the highest angel in heaven, or one single drop of water to the vast ocean. Let them consider, what a terrible sin and rashness it is, only to acknowledge Jesus Christ, the universal savior of the world, by whom all things in heaven and earth were created, and are to be reconciled, to be an actual savior and

---

67 "So those servants went out into the highways, and gathered together all as many as they found, both bad and good: and the wedding was furnished with guests. And when the king came in to see the guests, he saw there a man which had not on a wedding garment: And he saith unto him, Friend, how camest thou in hither not having a wedding garment? And he was speechless. Then said the king to the servants, Bind him hand and foot, and take him away, and cast him into outer darkness; there shall be weeping and gnashing of teeth. For many are called, but few are chosen." (Matt. 22:10-14).

68 "And he was angry, and would not go in: therefore came his father out, and intreated him. And he answering said to his father, Lo, these many years do I serve thee, neither transgressed I at any time thy commandment: and yet thou never gavest me a kid, that I might make merry with my friends: But as soon as this thy son was come, which hath devoured thy living with harlots, thou hast killed for him the fatted calf. And he said unto him, Son, thou art ever with me, and all that I have is thine. It was meet that we should make merry, and be glad: for this thy brother was dead, and is alive again; and was lost, and is found." (Luke 15:28-32).

Redeemer of about the thousandth part of mankind, and consequently rob him of almost all his glory, by leaving him for his
real property no more than that very small number or handful of
elect or first-born men unto salvation,[69] and by excluding all the
rest of the unspeakable multitude of men and creatures, to all
eternity, from any real participation of the tender mercy and love
of God, and the redemption of his beloved Son, although it evidently appears from Scripture to be designed for all. For, although it is too true, that a great part of mankind, like Esau, will,
through their own fault, be entirely deprived of, and lose the
great prerogative of their birth-right, and so far be castaway; yet
it is utterly false, that therefore they will be altogether excluded
from all enjoyments of the tender mercies of God, and be
doomed to endless torments, and never, never feel the virtue of
Christ's atoning blood. Can this be the perfect, ancient, and eternal Gospel, which Christ has commanded to be preached to every creature, or to the whole creation?[70] which his apostles
preached to every creature which is under heaven?[71] Yea, was it
this which Christ himself preached to the spirits in the infernal
prison, when he announced to them that the judgment passed
upon them had been only intended for the destruction of the
flesh, or that which was carnal, sinful, and diabolical in them,
but that they should live again according to God in the spirit?[72] I
can never believe this partial gospel to be that which Christ commanded to be preached to every creature, let who may, can, and
will; but I rather hold it, if not for a quite perverse and new, yet
at least for a corrupt, mutilated, and wrongfully circumscribed
gospel, contrived and introduced by depraved and self-wise human reason, in order to obscure and suppress the true gospel of

69   Matt. 22:14; Matt. 7:14
70   Mark 16:15
71   Col. 1:23
72   1 Pet. 3:19-20 compared with 1 Pet. 4:6

our eternal Redeemer, which alone has the power to make men godly and happy from the bottom of their hearts, when the other only serves to propagate bigotry, slavish fear, and hypocrisy. And I am apt to think, if even an angel from heaven was to preach the before-mentioned curtailed gospel to the zealous apostle Paul, who in his writings has left us the most excellent testimonies of the impartial and universal love of God, he would denounce an anathema against him.[73]

Therefore all such of every sect and religious party in Christendom, who will not suffer the true ancient gospel of Christ to be preached, which, according to our savior's plain words, is designed for every creature, but with all their might endeavor to suppress it, in order to establish the new invented, partial, and mutilated gospel, which hardly extends to a thousandth part of God's creatures; all such, I say, will have great reason to be afraid of the aforementioned anathema of the apostle Paul.

Those men discover a terribly envious spirit, and an intolerably diabolical pride, by grudging most creatures the endless mercy of God, and endeavoring totally to deprive them of it; but let them take care that thereby they do not incur the danger of being themselves for a long period excluded from the real enjoyment of it. This is certain, that in so doing, they commit a sin which deserves such a punishment.

For in the same manner as they behave towards their fellow creatures, that are in the estimation of God as good as themselves, even so will God behave himself towards them; and with the same measure that they mete unto their brethren, it shall be measured unto them; yea, good measure, pressed down, shaken together, and running over, shall be given into their bosom.[74] Let them reflect upon the terrible and just threatening which God has annexed as a conclusion to the book wherein he so plainly

---

73 Gal 1:8-9
74 Luke 6:38. See also to this purpose Matt. 18:33-35

declares, that every creature which is in heaven and on the earth, and under the earth, and such as are in the sea, and all that are in them, shall praise and glorify God and the Lamb for ever and ever;[75] and that he will make all things new.[76] He says, if any man shall take away from the words of the book of this prophecy, God shall take away his part out of the book of life, and out of the holy city, and from the things which are written in this book.[77]

Oh, how eagerly will all those upon whom this terrible judgment lights, wish that it may be true, what has been testified unto them of the everlasting riches of God's love; and that on the other hand, all opposite dogmas which convert the everlasting love of God into endless fury and wrath, though propagated by themselves in this world, may be false! But for their just punishment, they will have no full assurance, and consequently no comfort of it in their hearts, during all that terrible long period wherein God will entirely hide his face from them.[78]

If we ponder well our own natural wretchedness, and the condition we are in under the fall, it should, methinks, bring pretty low; nay, utterly destroy that pride and envy of ours, which causeth us to endeavor rashly to exclude from the everlasting mercy of God, so many millions of angelical and human creatures. For without the mercy of God, we are not only as bad as the most wicked wretch on earth, but we are also nothing better than the devil and his angels. Nay, one may in truth say, that man, in some measure, has discovered greater wickedness against God's most holy majesty than the devils themselves. For the evil spirits have never yet opposed God in endeavoring to work out their own salvation, because the economy and proper

---

75 Rev. 5:13
76 Rev. 21:5
77 Rev. 22:19
78 See Prov. 1:24–32

periods for it are not yet come, and consequently they have had no opportunity of committing this most heinous of all sins; though they have opposed God, and still continue to oppose him, in his endeavors to deliver mankind from their lower, and to translate them into the kingdom of his beloved Son; but this is hardly to be wondered at, considering the most depraved state they are in. But men, on the contrary, most vehemently resist the Holy Ghost in the work of their own salvation, from their youth, not only in ignorance, but too often knowingly and willfully. Not to mention, that things cannot go worse among the devils, in their dark infernal regions, than they go among men of this wicked world. Ah, what discord is there among them! How do they plague and torment one another! What contentions, quarrels, seditions, vexation and oppression of the poor and needy! What wars and bloodshed do we not continually hear of! But that this is not the case with the devils (of which men ought to be ashamed) and that they do not fall out among themselves our savior himself declares,[79] alleging at the same time the reason for it, because then their kingdom would not stand. There is another thing wherein men are frequently far more criminal than devils, and that is, in profane language, cursing, swearing, blaspheming, and execrating themselves: when an evil spirit spake to Jesus, with how much reverence he addressed him, "I know thee, who thou art, the Holy One of God!"[80] And far from execrating themselves, or wishing damnation to come upon them, as wicked men frequently do, they earnestly besought our Lord that he would not torment them nor send them into the abyss.[81]

So it clearly appears, that in many cases the iniquity of men surpasses that of the devils themselves. A truly penitent, afflicted and contrite heart would infallibly despair at this terrible sight of

79   Matt. 12:26
80   Mark 1:24
81   Mark 5:7; Luke 8:28-31

human wickedness, when it comes to have a full view thereof as well in itself as in others, if the universal and most impartial mercy of God in Jesus Christ our eternal Redeemer, and through his all-sufficient merits, was not its comfort.

In such a state men learn to set the true value upon the precious pearl of this evangelical truth, and begin to conceive that the origin of all railing against, and contradicting this blessed doctrine, is either that gross, or subtle Pharisaical spirit in mankind, that cannot so easily be rooted out, even in the disciples of Christ; and this spirit prevents men from knowing, feeling, and acknowledging that more than diabolical wickedness which lies in our corrupt nature, and consequently while under the government of such a temper, they can neither understand nor duly esteem that adequate and grand remedy designed by God for the curing and taking away of this great evil. So far indeed I allow a preference to fallen men before the apostate angels; that God offers his mercy first to men, since his justice requires that the deceived should be restored before the deceivers; but the ground for this preference does not lie in ourselves, but in the endless mercy and most holy justice of God. For in our depraved and corrupt estate, we need not imagine ourselves to be one whit better than the fallen angels, or to deserve the least preference before them.

That which makes them devils, and an abomination in God's eyes, namely, their perverse self-will, which will not bow under God, but would be entirely independent, not subject to the divine law; that same perverse self-will, is the thing in us which renders us as abominable in the sight of God as the fallen angels themselves. This perverse self-will is the true devil in all fallen sinful creatures, this is that which constitutes angels, devils, who otherwise would be good creatures of God. Hence, it is that such men as follow their perverse self-will (which may insinuate itself into the most sacred things) and suffer it to reign in themselves, and to prevail over them, are called in Scripture by the same names which are given to evil angels. They are for instance called adversaries, or Satans, which means the same.[82] Therefore all fallen men as far as they are under the dominion of sin, or their perverse self-will, are nothing else but *diaboli incarnati*, or incarnate devils. Whosoever will not know this, nor own himself to be according to the fallen nature as bad as the devil himself, such a one does not know as yet his sinful state as he ought to do; he is far from being rightly grounded in true humility, and there is as yet a great deal of the abominable seed of spiritual pride in his heart, let him think never so much of his holiness and humility. He has never yet begun truly and in reality to practice the earnest command of his savior, to hate himself or his own life,[83] (to wit, in his own corrupt nature, which deserves as much to be hated as the devil himself) and therefore does not know how to esteem sufficiently the everlasting mercy of God, and the precious blood of our universal Redeemer. For if he but knew the horrible wickedness of his own evil nature, and had come duly to esteem the endless mercies of God and all-sufficient merits of Christ, he really would not grudge one of the fallen creatures a part in the boundless love of God, and that grace of Jesus Christ which is able to deliver souls from hell, but would wish them all to partake of it as freely as he himself attained it, even if there was not one word of it mentioned in the Bible; whereas the Scripture abundantly testifies of this boundless, infinite, everlasting love, and the whole creation declares it to us as it were with living voices, if we would but hear it.

Now our ever-loving God, who has begun to have mercy on fallen men, who, in their sinful nature, are incarnate devils, and

---

82 Matt. 16:23; 1 Tim. 5:14. Yea, *diaboli*, that is devils, or calumniators, etc., John 6:70; 1 Tim. 3:6-7

83 Luke 14:86

has already made great numbers of them holy children of God, resembling the angels in heaven, and will continue so to do; the same ever-loving God, I say, will in his own time have pity also upon the rest of mankind, who in this life have forfeited their spiritual birthright; and not upon them only, but even on the fallen angels themselves, when they will begin to humble themselves truly before God. And then it will be as easy for him to make them holy angels again, as it was to make angel-like men and children of God of so many thousands of fallen men or incarnate devils. And that this will certainly come to pass in the fulness of the ages or periods appointed for it, will admit of no doubt, if we consider the promise of God, that he will make all things new.[84] And that he hath prepared all things that are in heaven, and on the earth for this renovation or actual reconciliation, by reconciling them to himself by the death of his Son, who hath made peace by the blood of his cross.[85]

To conclude, let us further consider, that it will be as easy a matter for the everlasting mercy of God to forgive the fallen angels their sins, whenever they will begin to humble themselves before him, as it is for him to forgive us ours. For let their sins be ever so great, ever so many, or ever so grievous, yet both have but one source, that is, as above said, self-will and pride. And as the nature of things does not admit of any other source of evil, so there is no other God, but he who himself is mercy and love.

---

84   Rev. 21:5
85   See Rom. 5:10; Col. 1:20

VI.

Of the everlasting Validity and Efficacy of the Merits of Christ, and the Eternal Redemption found out by Him; and that the same is infinitely more powerful than all Sin, and Corruption springing therefrom.

NONE, it is to be hoped, who claims the name of a Christian among all religious parties of Christendom, let them otherwise be never so much divided, will deny Christ, the Redeemer to be stronger and far more powerful than the devil, and the grace of redemption and salvation procured by him through his merits and sufferings to be infinitely more efficacious than all sin, together with the corruption and misery springing therefrom. For whosoever would deny this, would not only declare himself an infidel, but even a blasphemer against Christ. Besides, the nature of the thing requires it, that a savior or deliverer be stronger than the enemy whose prisoners he is to take away by force; and the plain word of God declares Jesus Christ to be such a savior and Deliverer.[86]

But there is a doctrine propagated and believed by many, which is quite inconsistent with what is advanced above; namely, "That although Christ has redeemed all men, or through his blood bought and reconciled them unto God, yet none really partake of his redemption but those who in this life believe in him, and by faith endure to the end; and that all the rest of mankind, who do not come to believe in Christ in this life, but continue in unbelief to the end of their days, will not only be terribly punished in the age to come," which is true, "but that they

---

86   See Isa. 49:25-26; Hos. 13:14; Luke 11:21-22; 1 John 4:4; Rom. 5:20

will, moreover, with all evil angels, be separated from God to all endless eternity, even so long as God shall exist, and shall suffer endless torments, and never share in the redemption of Christ."

How is it possible now, I pray, according to this doctrine, that Christ should be stronger than the devil? How can the grace procured and purchased by his merits, sufferings and death, be more efficacious than sin and all corruption and misery springing from it? For our savior declares in plain terms, and daily experience confirms it, that by far the smallest number of men find in their lifetime the narrow way of repentance and faith, and through the straight gate go into eternal life; but that, on the contrary, most of them go the broad way of perdition, and become a prey to the jaws of hell.[87] Ah! If no more men are really partakers of the redemption of Christ, than those, who in this life come to be united to him, he will hardly be a savior to the millionth part of mankind; and Satan will, according to his wish and pleasure, keep the greatest number captives in his empire to all endless eternity. And according to this scheme, how can Christ be said to be stronger than his enemy the devil? But you will perhaps reply, that the strength of Christ manifests itself, and may be known by his really delivering and snatching out of the jaws of Satan the few elect. But pray, is Christ to be only a savior of the elect? Is he not also a propitiation for the sins of the whole world?[88] And has he not bought with his blood those who bring upon themselves swift destruction?[89]

If a man was to give out of himself against his enemy, who had led a million of his people captive, that he was stronger than such an enemy, and that he would heat and spoil him of all his prisoners, because he heartily pitied the poor souls; and coming thereupon to the battle, was to deliver, of a million of prisoners,

---

87   See Matt. 7:13-14; Luke 13:23-24; Matt. 22:14
88   1 John 2:2
89   2 Pet. 2:1

about three, or at the most ten, leaving all the rest in slavery, because the enemy had too well secured them; pray, would you believe such a man to be much stronger than his enemy, since of a million of prisoners, he had actually delivered about three or ten? Would you not be apt to say, that he had boasted much more of himself than he was able to perform, and justly conclude, that he must want either strength or power to overcome the enemy, or mercy and compassion towards the poor captives? Now, such a bragging, yea, unmerciful, or infirm man do we generally make of Christ, by teaching and acknowledging on the one hand, that he is a universal Redeemer, but on the other hand, perversely pretend, that but the smallest number of men, viz. the few elect (who, compared to the rest of mankind, are hardly as ten to a million) in reality partake of his redemption, and that all the residue of fallen men and other creatures are to be wholly excluded therefrom to all endless eternity. Certainly if Christ is no other than such a savior to as, I say again, the devil, who according to the common opinion, will forever, world without end, and as long as Christ is to be Christ, keep in his power and under his dominion by far the greatest part of men, of whom we at the same time own that Christ has an earnest desire to redeem them, must be many thousand times mightier than he. Verily if this was the case with our Redeemer, he must either fall short of power to conquer the devil, or want pity and compassion towards those poor souls that are kept prisoners by the devil.

Maybe you will make me another objection, and say, that Christ neither wants for force to conquer his enemy, nor mercy towards the captives; but that the reason why so few men are really delivered by him, is, because they resist his grace, and spontaneously desire to remain the infernal tyrant's slaves. To this I answer, But what is then such resistance and obstinacy in most men against the grace of Jesus Christ offered them? What is the blindness and hardness of their hearts, according to which they themselves choose to continue in the service of the devil? Are they not altogether the workings of Satan? Are they not all chains and snares wherewith he has bound and entangled poor men? Now if Christ, who is to be a universal savior of mankind, will in most men never, to all endless eternity, and as long as God is to remain God, destroy such works of the devil; if he will never break and untie the chains and fetters wherewith Satan hath bound the greatest part of mankind; it will still follow, that Christ must be either unmerciful, and not willing to do it, or that he is not able to perform what he would desire. But how absurd, nay, how great a blasphemy is it to make the devil, and that which is evil, stronger than Christ, and that which is good, and sin more powerful than the grace of God? Thanks be to God, that in Christ we have such a Redeemer, who, although he is a special savior of those that believe,[90] because he will grant them to sit with him upon his throne,[91] and make them partakers of all his glories, to which dignity and high degree of salvation, none of those will ever attain who must be humbled and brought to Christ by the judgment of the next age; yet he is nevertheless not a mere titular, but a real savior of all the rest of men; who also by the blood of his covenant sendeth forth his prisoners out of the pit, wherein is no water,[92] that is out of the state of the damned, where not one drop of comfort is to be found. He has the keys of hell, and of death,[93] and consequently is able to cast into, and discharge therefrom whomsoever he pleases; and he will actually ransom them from the power of the grave (or hell) and will redeem them from death, in such a manner, as to be a plague to death, and total destruction to the grave (or hell).[94] That is, he

90 1 Tim. 4:10
91 Rev. 3:21
92 Zech. 9:11
93 Rev. 1:18
94 Hos. 13:14

will continue so long to redeem from hell, till not one prisoner more shall be left in its jaws and in the power of the devil, and death, and all the power of Satan shall be destroyed and wholly annihilated. Then shall be completely fulfilled what is written:

> "Death is swallowed up in victory. Oh, death where is thy sting! Oh, grave (or hell) where is thy victory! The sting of death is sin, and the strength of sin is the law. But thanks be to God, who giveth us the victory through our Lord Jesus Christ."[95] (1 Cor. 4:54-57)

If but one soul was to remain in the power of the devil, death, or hell, to all endless eternity, as long as God shall exist, then the devil, death, and hell, would forever have something to boast of against God, and to upbraid him with not being able really to spoil them of all their prisoners, to the very last, but that he was obliged to leave them something, and consequently give up the conquest to them. And thus death would not be entirely swallowed up in victory to all endless eternity, but would always keep something of his sting; and hell would not quite lose the field of battle, but would be forevermore able to make a scorn of those who should say, hell, where is thy victory? For it might at least boast of one soul of which Christ could not deprive it, though he had shed his blood for it. With how much more right now could the devil, death and hell, mock Christ and his believers, if they were to ask them, "O death, where is thy sting? O hell, where is thy victory?" in case these enemies could (according to the common pretense, whereof the Scripture knows nothing) keep at pleasure the greatest part of mankind for their prisoners as long as God shall exist? It is plain that by Christ, the universal savior, all captivated men are to be actually snatched out of the power of the devil and his angels; and this, when it is

95   1 Cor. 4:54–57

fully accomplished, will be an occasion to oblige Lucifer and his angels also to humble themselves entirely before Christ Jesus, which (except the incarnation of our savior, and what he did and suffered on earth to work out the salvation of his creatures) will be the greatest wonder that ever was wrought in the creation. And this the Holy Scripture clearly foretells, when it says, that all things under the earth, that is, not only damned men, but even the fallen spirits, shall at last bow the knee in the name of Jesus, and confess with their inmost heart as well as tongue, that He, and not Satan, is Lord, to the glory of God the Father.[96]

Then they, together with all the rest of creatures, shall praise God with loud hallelujahs and inexpressible joy.[97]

For, when now the whole armor of this strong man shall be taken from him, and all his spoils divided, that is, all men who were made a prey of by him, restored to God, and brought again to the company of his saints, and Satan be thus entirely conquered by Christ, and reduced to the condition of a king without subjects or dominions, what then will he do else, but after the manner of an utterly routed enemy, be obliged to prostrate himself before his conqueror, and pray for mercy! And this total subduing will make way for the restoration of Lucifer and his angels.

For, as the most high God could not have mercy upon them, nor could deliver them out of their most wretched condition, as long as through pride they wanted to be like him, or even above him; so may they be helped when all the stays of their pride are consumed, and reduced to ashes in the lake of fire and brimstone, and of proud and haughty devils they have become humbled spirits, that bow down in the dust before God and Christ, praying for mercy: for God resisteth only the proud, and without

---

96   Phil. 2:10-11
97   See Rev. 5:13 compared with Psalm 145:9–11; Psalm 150:6

the least respect of person, giveth grace to all humble creatures.[98]

Although the offer of God's grace in the said manner will be very acceptable news to Lucifer and his angels, at the time of their deepest abasement and humiliation by Christ (which doubtless will yet require many thousand years); nevertheless the doctrine of his restoration, and the means for it, are, in his present situation, not at all agreeable to him; but the distant prophecies of his subjection are to him most dreadful tidings. For as he is a proud and haughty spirit to the highest degree, who is by no means willing to be subject to God, but would fain be his equal, or rather above him, who with all his might opposes, and if possible, would dethrone the Most High; therefore it is intolerable for him to be foretold, according to divine truth, that by Christ all his power, his whole empire, and all his subjects, not one excepted, shall be taken from him, and he himself brought down so low as to lie in the dust like a vile worm before Christ, and to worship him; which at present he would reckon his greatest shame, and would much rather that Christ and his followers, together with the rest of mankind, should worship him, or take his will for their law. Therefore is this gospel a most frightful lecture to him, to hear that once he shall be entirely thrown down from his high places, and brought again into the right order of God's creatures, which is humility and subjection under God and Christ.[99]

That the doctrine that Christ will entirely vanquish the devil, is intolerable to him, the following parable may serve to illustrate.

Suppose a poor, miserable, naked beggar man, was to be presented to a grand, proud, and tyrannical monarch in the world, who was in possession of a vast empire, having many millions of subjects; and it should be foretold him by divine authority, that

98   1 Pet. 5:5; Isa. 57:15
99   Eph. 1:10

this man, so worthless and contemptible in his eyes, should one day or another, conquer his whole empire and strip him of all his subjects, so that at last he would be obliged to fall down naked at his feet, to acknowledge him his lord, and depend on his mercy; can anyone imagine this would be an agreeable prophecy to the said grand, proud and tyrannical monarch! Would he not rather fret and fume, and treat them in the most barbarous manner, as mutineers and rebels, who should foretell such a revolution? An instance of this we see in Herod, he only supposing in a foolish manner, that Jesus the new-born King of the Jews, might be a rival to him and his sons, what cruel means he made use of to prevent the imaginary mischief![100] Now the doctrine of the restoration of all creatures, is a thousand times more terrible news to the devil; by which he is foretold, that Jesus, that most despised and rejected one,[101] who when he dwelt on earth was despised and abhorred, whom Satan, through his instruments, did in the most terrible manner revile, mock, spit upon, persecute and torment; and who is still abused in his name, character, and followers, by the children of the devil: that he, I say, shall at last conquer the whole empire of Satan, spoil him of all his subjects and dominions, and oblige him to fall at his feet, who once was numbered with the transgressors,[102] and worship him in the humblest manner.

In short, this doctrine tends utterly to destroy the kingdom of the devil, and all that is diabolical, such as pride, envy, and fury; and therefore the hearing of it, must be the greatest mortification to Satan imaginable.

From what has been said, it may easily be concluded, that it is no wonder if Satan is enraged against this holy gospel, and endeavors with all his power to suppress it, using especially for his

---

100 See Matt. 2
101 See Isa. 53:3
102 Isa. 53:12

instruments the hypocritical Pharisees of this age, false theologians, and the naturally and legally pious people, and such as are but half converted, whose minds are not yet free from wrath, and who look upon God as an endless furious being towards all his creatures, because their souls had never yet a due sense of his infinite love and mercy towards all his works. Nay, I am afraid that even many, otherwise well-meaning souls, will be stirred up to fight against this holy doctrine, particularly those who hold the traditions of their fathers for indisputably divine truths, which they have been obliged to swear to, and call them the hedge about the Lord's vineyard: for finding some of them diametrically opposite to this blessed gospel of the universal and impartial love of God, they will perhaps be enticed to declare it to be fanaticism, and a long condemned heresy, which they think themselves obliged to guard again?? But if the whole world, and all those that are reckoned the wisest and most pious, were to rise up against it, this holy truth will, nevertheless, make its way through all opposition, and be applauded by the children of truth.

Ye that stigmatize the propagators of this doctrine in the world, do but consider what is represented thereby! It is the most tender and at the same time most just mercy of our God, whereby the day spring from on high hath visited us; in order to give also at last light to them that sit in darkness and in the shadow of death, and to guide our feet into the way of peace![103] Pray what harm can this do? You may protest against it as much as you please, the words of Solomon's song on our side, describing the majesty of the love of God, will nevertheless be found true, viz.:

"Love is strong as death, jealousy is cruel (or hard) as
the grave (or hell, to give it battle, and carry the day)

103 Luke 1:78-79

the coals thereof are coals of fire, which hath a most
vehement flame. Many waters cannot quench love,
neither can the floods drown it; if a man would give
all the substance of his house for love, it would utterly
be contemned."[104] (Songs 8:6-7)

Now, as the representation of God's universal and everlasting love must, for the above-mentioned reasons, be hateful to the malevolent devil; so on the contrary, that doctrine cannot but very much please him, which teaches that he will to all eternity, or while God exists, keep, as his subjects and slaves, the far greater part of mankind, though purchased by the blood of Jesus our savior; which consequently, according to his wish and pleasure, in general, and very near entirely sets at nought the intent of Christ's redemption, and the divine love and mercy manifested thereby. And which teaches that the greatest part of mankind, and all the fallen angels, shall always continue rebels in heart against God, without ever being brought down in true humility to worship God and Christ in spirit and in truth; for the Father seeketh such to worship him, and will have no other subjects and worshipers than such as those.[105]

---

104 Songs 8:6-7
105 John 4:23-24

VII.

OF THE WORD ETERNITY, AND THE DIFFERENT ETERNITIES, OR AGES, MENTIONED IN THE SCRIPTURES.

THE words forever, for ever and ever, everlasting, eternal, expressed in the Hebrew language by *ad olam, olamim*; and in the Greek language *aion, aionios, aionion, eis tous aionas ton aionon*, etc., have not always the same, but different significations in the Holy Scriptures, as is well known to the learned.

We may say, that in general, these words are used for every long and hidden duration or continuance of things, whether this duration be final and endless; or of such a nature, that, as it is not without beginning, rooted in the everlasting and incorruptible being of God, and his creating power, but has had its beginning from the creature, and so must of necessity cease at last, and have an end; or infinite, that is of such a nature that, as it had no beginning, either in respect to the real existence or being of the thing itself, or in regard to its root and origin, so necessarily has no end, or may at least be without end or any cessation.

Therefore, whenever we find the word eternal, or everlasting, in the Holy Scriptures, we are not immediately to conclude that an absolutely endless duration must be intended; but we ought first of all to look upon the nature and property of the things that are said to be eternal or everlasting, and consider whether their nature will admit of an endless, or only of a limited duration, and explain the word everlasting accordingly.

That this is a true and irrefutable rule to be observed, in all explanations and expositions, we are taught, as school-boys, by the canon of logic; saying, *prædicata, intelligenda runt secundum substratum materiam;* or, *talia sunt prædicata, qualia permittuntur esse a suis subjectis*; that is, "that what is said of a thing must be understood in such a manner as the nature of the thing will allow of." Such, for instance, is the term power, which is lodged in one person to command, or rule others. For this power is not the same in all persons that have any command or government; it being of one kind in an absolute emperor, monarch or king, and of another in a prince, and it is still different in an earl, count, baron, or gentleman. Nay, power may be different in a mayor or magistrate of a city, from that in a justice of the peace in the country; and yet there is some kind of power in all these. So it is with respect to the word forever, or everlasting; all things which the Holy Spirit, in the sacred Scriptures, call everlasting, are, in a sense, really so, that is, they have such an existence and duration as is grounded on their nature, and especially on the will of God. For this the word everlasting really signifies, and nothing else, as I shall endeavor to show incontestably before I have done. For the word everlasting is of a quite different extent when it is used to express the duration of the being of God, than when it is attributed to those creatures that have their being from God, and to the good which is derived from him; and again, it is still different when it is applied to sin, and the evil of punishment depending thereon, as coming from the creature alone without God. Now, if I say that the word eternal, when applied to God in the Scriptures, signifies an absolutely endless duration, because, God having no beginning, can have no end; and that when it is used of the creatures that have their being from God, as also of their good and blessed condition which they derive from him, it then signifies such an eternal duration, which, as to the real existence or being of things, has had its beginning, but is, or may be, without end; because God, in whose incorruptible, creating power, such things are rooted, has neither beginning nor end. If any should infer from hence, that the word eternal, or everlasting, must also signify an absolutely endless duration, when it is used to express the continuance of sin and the evil of punishment depending thereon, in this and the next state; such a conception would be more absurd than it would be to imagine the power of a country justice of the peace to be the same with that of an absolute monarch or king.

Therefore to form a true and distinct idea of the words forever, for ever and ever, everlasting, and eternal, wherever they occur in Scripture, we have to observe, that all the eternities or ages mentioned therein, are chiefly divided into three sorts, and may be distinguished accordingly; as in some measure appears from the preceding paragraph, and is well known to people of understanding.

The last sort of eternities mentioned in Scripture, may be called *Æternitas absolute infinita a parte ante et post*, that is, an absolutely endless eternity; or, such a duration as has neither beginning nor end. This is always the meaning of the word eternal or everlasting, when it is applied to the Divine Being and his attributes; since God is Jehovah, or that supreme self-existent Being, which, as he never had a beginning, but has been in and of himself from everlasting, giving all other things their existence, so neither can he ever have an end.

> *"And Abraham planted a grove in Beersheba, and called there on the name of Jehovah, the everlasting God."*[106] *(Gen. 21:33)*

> *"Jehovah shall reign for ever and ever."*[107] *(Exod. 15:18)*

---

106 Gen 21:33
107 Exod. 15:18

*"Before the mountains were brought forth, or ever
thou hadst formed the earth and the world; even from
everlasting to everlasting thou art God."[108] (Psalm
90:2)*

*"Thy throne is established of old; thou art from
everlasting."[109] (Psalm 93:2)*

*"But Jehovah is the true God; he is the living God, and
an everlasting King."[110] (Jer. 10:10)*

*"And when those living animals give glory, and honor,
and thanks to him that sat on the throne, who liveth
for ever and ever, the four and twenty elders fall down
before him that sat on the throne, and worship him
that liveth for ever and ever"[111], etc. (Rev. 4:9-10)*

The second sort of ages or eternities that the Holy Scriptures speak of, we may call *Æternitas infinita a parta post*; that is, such an endless eternity or duration, which, although it has a beginning, yet will never have an end. This is intended by the word everlasting, when it is applied to the existence of those rational creatures which God hath made, and to the good which comes from God. Such is, for instance, the beatitude and glory of believers in the world to come. For, although the good that is to be found in the creatures, together with their existence, as distinct beings, has not always been, but has had a beginning, nevertheless it has absolutely an eternal root in God, in his almighty and incorruptible creating power, which is as ancient as God himself, because it is the same with God; and therefore his creatures,

108 Psalm 90:2
109 Psalm 93:2
110 Jer. 10:10
111 Rev. 4:9-10

which, according to his wisdom, by his power, and for his pleasure, he hath created, may, and doubtless shall be preserved in
existence to all ages, or while God exists, and their final state of
happiness shall be of the same duration.

> "Israel shall be saved in Jehovah with an everlasting
> salvation; ye shall not be ashamed nor confounded
> world without end."[112] (Isa. 45:17)

> "And they that be wise shall shine as the brightness of
> the firmament, and they that turn many to
> righteousness, as the stars for ever and ever."[113] (Dan.
> 12:3)

> "That whosoever believeth in him should not perish,
> but have eternal life. For God so loved the world, that
> he gave his only begotten Son, that whosoever
> believeth in him should not perish, but have
> everlasting life."[114] (John 3:15-16)

> "He that believeth on the Son hath everlasting life."[115]
> (John 3:36)

> "The water that I shall give him shall be in him a well
> of water springing up into everlasting life."[116] (John
> 4:14)

> "Verily, verily, I say unto you, he that heareth my
> word, and believeth on him that sent me, hath

---

112 Isa. 45:17
113 Dan. 12:3
114 John 3:15-16
115 John 3:36
116 John 4:14

everlasting life, and shall not come into condemnation, but is passed from death to life."[117] (John 5:24)

"labor not for the meat which perisheth, but for that meat which endureth unto everlasting life."[118] (John 6:27)

"And this is the will of him that sent me, that every one who seeth the Son, and believeth on him, may have everlasting life: and I will raise him up at the last day."[119] (John 6:40)

"Verily, verily, I say unto you, he that believeth on me hath everlasting life."[120] (John 6:47)

"Whoso eateth my flesh and drinketh my blood hath eternal life; and I will raise him up at the last day."[121] (John 6:54)

"Lord, to whom shall we go? thou hast the words of eternal life."[122] (John 6:68)

"And I give unto them eternal life; and they shall never perish, neither shall any pluck them out of my hand."[123] (John 10:28)

"He that loveth his life shall lose it, and he that hateth

117 John 5:24
118 John 6:27
119 John 6:40
120 John 6:47
121 John 6:54
122 John 6:68
123 John 10:28

his life in this world shall keep it unto life eternal."[124]
(John 12:25)

"And I know that his (the Father's) commandment is
life everlasting."[125] (John 12:50)

"As thou hast given him power over all flesh that he
should give eternal life to as many as thou hast given
him."[126] (John 17:2)

"And this is life eternal, that they might know thee,
the only true God, and Jesus Christ whom thou hast
sent."[127] (John 17:3)

All these passages, and many more that might be brought, intend the second kind of eternities or ages: viz. those that have a
beginning, but shall never have an end.

The third sort of eternities mentioned in the Holy Scriptures,
may be called *Æternitas periodica*; that is, such an age or duration of things which is limited within a certain period of time,
longer or shorter, that has its certain beginning and end; since
the things to which such an *aion*, or forever, are ascribed are not
to last to an endless duration. In this sense the words forever, everlasting, etc. are very frequently used in the Scriptures, both of
the Old and New Testament.

Here we will only allege some of the plainest and chiefest
places. As for instance, the Holy Spirit calls a man's life-time
here on earth an eternity, or forever.[128]

Secondly, the Levitical priesthood, and divine worship of the

---

124 John 12:25
125 John 12:50
126 John 17:2
127 John 17:3
128 Exod. 21:6; Deut 15:17; 1 Sam. 1:22; Phil. 15

Old Testament, which was instituted by God only for a certain time, viz. until the time of Reformation, as the Holy Ghost expresses it,[129] that is, until the coming of Christ, who is the end of the law. This time, or period, is called an eternity, or forever, in the following passages: Exod. 12:14-17; Exod. 27:21; Exod. 28:43; Exod. 24:28; Exod. 30:21; Exod. 31:16-17; Exod. 40:15; Lev. 3:17; Lev. 4:13, Lev. 4:18; Lev. 4:22; Lev. 7:34; Lev. 7:36; Lev. 10:9; Lev. 10:15; Lev. 16:29; Lev. 16:31; Lev 16:34; Lev. 17:7; Lev. 23:14; Lev. 23:21; Lev. 23:31; Lev. 23:41; Lev. 24:3; Lev. 24:9; Numb. 10:8; Numb. 15:15; Numb. 18:8; Numb 18:11; Numb. 18:19; Numb 18:23; Numb. 19:10; Numb. 25:13; Deut. 18:5.

These are all said to be forever, everlasting, or perpetual, and yet were only for a certain period, as is evident to all Christians.

Thirdly, the time before Christ's incarnation, and the preaching of the Gospel by the apostles, in the whole world, is called the eternal age (*chronois aioniois*).[130]

And the apostle says that Christ appeared in the end of the eternity, or age (*ton aionon*).[131]

Fourthly, in general, and in a complex sense, the periods of time, or the ages, both of this present and the next world, which in some measure both subsist together, and succeed one another, and being linked like one chain, and reach even unto that eternity, when the Son of God, after the consummation of all his works, shall deliver up the kingdom to his Father, and himself, though without the least diminution of his glory, be subject unto him who put all things under him, that God may be all in all, in that only endless and still eternity of God, into which at last, all limited or periodical eternities shall be changed; or, in the sweetest manner return, as into the head-spring from which they

---

129 Heb. 9:10
130 Rom. 16:8-5
131 Heb. 9:26

flowed.[132]

Fifthly, this present wicked world or age, which is to have an end at the coming of Christ, is called by the same word that is rendered elsewhere forever, or eternity: Matt. 12:32; Matt. 13:22; Matt. 13:39; Matt. 13:40; Matt. 13:49; Matt. 24:3; Matt. 28:20; Mark 4:19; Luke 1:70; Luke 16:8; Luke 20:34; John 9:32; Acts 3:21; Acts 15:18; Rom. 12:2; 1 Cor. 1:20; 1 Cor. 2:6-7; 1 Cor. 3:18; 1 Cor. 8:13; 1 Cor. 10:11; 2 Cor. 4:4; Gal. 1:4; Eph. 1:21; Eph. 6:12; 1 Tim. 6:17; 2 Tim. 1:9; 2 Tim. 4:10; Tit. 1:2; Tit. 2:12.[133]

---

132 Heb. 11:3 compared with Eph. 1:21; Eph. 2:7; 1 Cor. 15:28; Rev. 11:15

133 N.B. In all these last places of Scripture, the English translation now in use has the word world, but the Greek original has the word *aion*, or some of its derivatives, which is nothing like world, but properly signifies the present age, which must end, though it is called by the same name which is applied to the life to come, and is rendered forever, or eternity; but whereby, in these places, can be understood nothing more than the duration or continuance of the time of this wicked age of the world, which is only to last till the coming of Christ.

VIII.

TO WHICH SORT OF ETERNITIES THE ETERNITY OF THE EVIL, AND THE PUNISHMENT DEPENDING THEREON, ETERNAL DAMNATION, AS IT IS CALLED, BELONGS.

As soon as evil or sin is severed from the creatures, the punishment thereof ceases.

For sin is the sting of death.[134] Now when this sting comes to be destroyed, then the pain and wounding of death discontinues too; as a fire must go out as soon as it wants combustibles.

On the contrary, so long as evil, or sin, subsists in the creatures, either within or without, or at least within, so long the punishment of sin will continue upon them both in this and the next world: so long will the wrath of God abide on them; for his indignation resteth upon sinners, so long as they continue in sin.

"He that believeth not is condemned already, because he hath not believed in the name of the only begotten Son of God."[135] (John 3:18)

"He that believeth not the Son shall not see life; but the wrath of God abideth on him."[136] (John 3:36)

"God is angry with the wicked every day."[137] (Psalm 7:11)

---

134 1 Cor. 15:56
135 John 3:18
136 John 3:36
137 Psalm 7:11

"Suffer not thy mouth to cause thy flesh to sin: neither say thou before the angel that it was an error: wherefore should God be angry at thy voice, and destroy the works of thine hands!"[138] *(Eccles. 5:6)*

Now, since many thousands of millions of the fallen creatures do not only go on in wickedness to the end of their days in this world, but will also be wicked in the world to come; so it follows that not only in this world or age, but particularly in that which is to come, as being under the severe but just judgment of God, they must be punished according to their deeds done in the body.

Many and terrible are the plagues and punishments which God often in this world inflicts on wicked creatures; but they are nothing to those punishments and torments that will come upon them hereafter. The Scriptures speak of them in the most dreadful terms and phrases, which are enough to make one's hair stand erect. But ah! how horrid and insupportable will they be to endure in reality![139]

But the punishments of the wicked creatures in the future state will not only be terrible beyond description, but they will also last eternally, that is, they will be of a true *aionion* duration, according to their nature. Therefore, as I do sincerely believe an eternal happiness, so sincerely do I believe an eternal damnation; that is, a future condemnation of the wicked, to those punishments of the next world which according to the dialect of the

---

138 Eccles. 5:6
139 See Deut. 32:34-35; Deut. 32:40-41; Psalm 7:12-13; Psalm 11:6; Psalm 73:17–20; Isa. 30:33; Isa. 33:14; Isa. 50:11; Isa. 65:13–15; Isa. 66:24; Ezek. 22:14; Matt. 3:12; Matt. 5:22; Matt. 5:29; Matt. 5:30; Matt. 7:19; Matt. 10:28; Matt. 13:40–42; Matt. 13:49; Matt. 13:50; Matt. 18:8-9; Matt. 18:34; Matt. 13:14; Matt. 13:33; Matt. 24:51; Matt. 25:30; Matt. 25:41; Matt. 25:46; Mark 3:29; Mark 9:42–49; Luke 12:46–48; Luke 13:25–28; Luke 16:23–26; 2 Thess. 1:8-9; Heb. 2:2-3; Heb. 6:8; Heb. 10:29–31; 1 Pet. 4:17-18; 2 Pet. 2:8; 2 Pet. 2:17; 2 Pet. 3:7; Jude 13–15; Rev. 14:10-11; Rev. 19:3; Rev. 19:20; Rev. 20:10; Rev. 20:14-15; Rev. 21:8; Rev. 22:15; Rev. 22:18-19

Holy Ghost, may be justly called eternal or *aionion*.[140] So that in truth no person can accuse me of denying that eternal damnation, wherewith God in his word, has threatened the wicked, without sinning against the ninth commandment, which if anyone does, I heartily pray God to forgive him.

But since the very same Spirit of Truth, which so very solemnly threatens the devils and all hardened sinners with eternal damnation, doth also on the other hand in holy writ, with great emphasis testify of God's everlasting and unbounded love towards all his creatures of the eternal and general redemption of our savior, and, in short, of the final renovation and restoration of all corrupt creatures, and consequently of their universal and happy subjection in the kingdom of God and of Christ, where every creature shall praise God: as has been already shown, and shall be most clearly demonstrated in the 12th chapter of this treatise, you must think that as a simple scholar of heavenly wisdom, I am obliged to take both for divine and consistent truths. And therefore I reckon the eternity of evil, and the punishment depending thereon, neither to the first, nor to the second, but to the third sort of eternities described in the foregoing chapter; because such evil, and the punishment thereof, has no everlasting root in God (as the creatures themselves, and the good that is imparted to them by God have), but is of the creatures, and during the created ages sprung up in them of their own creaturely will.

It may be some will say, that the protestations that I believe an eternal damnation, art nothing but a mere pretense and play-work, since my maintaining the Restoration of all things obliges me to believe that such eternal damnation must at last come to an end, and that consequently, my pretended true eternity of punishments in the next world, is no eternity at all. To this I an-

---

140 See Matt. 3:12; Matt. 18:8; Matt. 25:41; Matt. 25:46; Mark 3:29; Mark 9:43–48; 2 Thess. 1:9; Jude 7; Rev. 14:11; Rev. 19:3; Rev. 20:10

swer, that no man, let him he whosoever he will, must pretend to set up for a reformer of the language of the eternal wisdom of God, which calls *olamim, aionas* or eternities, not only the absolutely endless duration of the Divine being himself, and of those things which may subsist in him without end, but also such durations of things which are bounded within certain periods of time, as has been fully proved in the preceding chapter, so that the matter is as clear as day-light.

Can the Spirit of Truth justly call a man's life-time on earth, an *aiona*, age, forever, or eternity, which very often falls short of fifty years? With how much more justice may he call that period eternity, wherein the evil angels and men, shall, by a just judgment, be banished from the presence of God; which doubtless will contain our short life-time many hundreds of times multiplied? For which reason also, this frightful, long, but just period of the manifested wrath of God, is called in some places of Scripture, not merely *aion*, or eternity; but is expressed by *aionas ton ainon*, that is age of ages, or eternity of eternities.[141] Lord God preserve us from all this eternity! It will be too long to those that come into it, and we have no occasion, contrary to truth, to make it still longer than the Spirit of Truth hath made it.

Some pretend, that the eternity of evil, and the eternal damnation depending thereon, must be an absolutely endless eternity, and last as long as the being of God himself, because it is in some places of Scripture compared with the eternal happiness of the children of God, and its duration expressed in the same words; so that if the eternity of damnation was to cease, we must conclude that of eternal glory must have an end too.[142]

As plausible as this objection seems to be, so empty it is, if we go to the bottom thereof. We will at present answer to it, first, that all such as advance this objection against the eternal and

141 Rev. 14:14; Rev. 19:3; Rev. 20:10
142 Matt. 25:46; Rev. 14:11; Rev. 19:3; Rev. 20:10 compared with Rev. 11:15; Rev. 22:5

universal redemption, turn their own weapon against themselves, and unknowingly participate of a great error, which they will never own themselves to be guilty of; for, let these people only consider, that if we are obliged to conclude, according to their opinion, that the eternity of pain and the eternity of glory must be of an exactly equal extent and length, because they are both compared together in the Scriptures, and their duration is expressed in the same words; then it must also necessarily follow, that the evil and punishment depending thereon, must have been from all eternity, and either without any beginning at all, or must at least have an endless root in God, and consequently be itself God, or his creature. This latter is the case with the eternal glory and happiness. For, although the creature's real enjoyment of the eternal happiness and glory begins here in time, yet the eternal happiness and glory, or the glorious kingdom of God itself, is without any beginning, and existed in and with God, ever since God himself has been, that is, from all inconceivable eternity; and must therefore, certainly, exist so long as God himself, who is the only source of all true beatitude and glory, shall exist.[143]

If the eternity of evil is in every respect to answer to the extension of the eternity of glory in and with God, then the extension of the eternity of evil, must be backwards as well as forwards, and consequently has been from all inconceivable eternity, and ever since God himself has existed; the holding of which would resemble the heresy of the ancient Manicheans, as much as one egg does another.

Again, if anyone would say, that the equality of these two eternities, of evil and of good, is not backwards, but forwards, that is, although evil, to wit, sin and punishment depending thereon, was not without beginning, as the eternal happiness,

---

143 See Matt. 25:34 compared with Eph. 1:4

considered in itself, and according to its nature was; yet that the eternity of evil is without end; and forwards, of the same extension with the eternity of glory; he must know, that if this extension is not to be the same, as well backwards as forwards, it wants a great deal of being every way alike; and, if my adversary is obliged, to avoid falling into heresy, to shorten it one way, why should not I have liberty, for good and weighty reasons, to cut it short another way? I answer, secondly, that it is altogether false that the Scripture always, whenever it uses the words *aion, aionios,* or forever, of two contrary things, thereby necessarily understands an equally long duration of both. I will here only allege three plain passages of Scripture which prove the contrary. Please to look into the Greek text of Matt. 12:32; Luke 20:34-35; Eph. 1:21. In these places this present world, and the future, or next world, are compared together, where it is said in the Greek, according to the Scripture style, *en touto to aioni, oute en to mellonti; ton aionos toutou, ton aionos ekinou; en to aioni toutou, en to mellonti;* that is, this eternity, or age, and the eternity, or age to come. But by this eternity, or age, nothing else is meant but this world, or the present period of time, which has begun with the fall of man, and will end with the coming of Christ; and by the next world is intended that period of Christ's future reign in his manifested glory. But if by the words *aion, aionios,* eternity, or eternal, we are always to understand an equally long duration, even when they are used of contrary things, it must necessarily follow from the above quoted texts of Scripture, that the future world, wherein Christ is foreign in his glory, is to last no longer than this present wicked world; for the periods of both worlds are expressed by the Holy Spirit, according to his usual way of speaking, by one and the same word, namely, *aion,* eternity, or age, as is also the duration of the future damnation and happiness.[144] But who of the opposers of the Restoration of all things will allow of this, especially as long as by the future world they understand an endless eternity, according to the common hypothesis?

Thirdly and lastly, if our adversaries will absolutely have it so, that the glorious reign of Christ with his elect, and the state of damnation and unhappiness of the poor creatures cast into the fiery lake, must be two equally long eternities, and we should even grant them this too, they would gain nothing at all by it against the blessed doctrine of the Restoration. That economy, therefore, and sort of government of Christ and his elect, during which all enemies must be put under Christ's feet, and all rebellious creatures in reality made subject unto God and Christ, after the abolition of death, and sin which is the sting of death; that economy, I say, will certainly have an end; namely, at that period when Christ's aim is obtained, and the Son himself shall be subject to Him that put all his under his feet. But hereby is not meant that the kingdom of Christ shall cease, which, according to the word of God is to have no end.[145] But it will rather through such subjection of Christ under God his Father, get an infinitely greater lustre. So that we must well distinguish between the particular government of Christ and his elect, and the kingdom of Christ and his believers as one with the kingdom of his heavenly Father.

The first will certainly cease, and consequently the eternities of eternities, or ages of ages, appointed for it will end; but the latter is to last forevermore, or to all eternity.

Now, as long as the said eternities or ages of the particular government of Christ are to last and succeed one another, so long will also last the eternities or ages of pain in the fiery lake: for as soon as all eternities are conquered, and every creature is

---

144 Matt. 25:46
145 Luke 1:33

brought to true obedience and subjection under God and Christ, he will deliver up the kingdom to the Father. Therefore, both these eternities are of an exactly like long duration.

IX.

Of the different sorts or degrees of damnation: that is, of the first and second Death, or the Prisons of the Sea, Death, Hell and the Fiery Lake.

ALL punishing justice, if it be worthy of the name of justice, requires that the punishment be in proportion and according to the nature of the sin, and the situation of the sinner. So we find that even in this world a righteous judge inflicts no greater punishment on a malefactor than his crime deserves; nay, his severest punishments are usually mitigated, and mixed with some mercy.

Now, since those men, who in their unaltered sinful condition are carried off into the other world, and after their departure abide under the wrath of God,[146] are not all alike wicked, but some have sinned a great deal more than others, and consequently, through the growth of their inward iniquity have become more conformable unto the devil than others; so it follows of itself, that the punishments which the Divine justice will inflict upon the depraved creatures in the next world, will be unequal, and in proportion to the heinousness and greatness of their crimes; some punishments being very severe and long, and others more tolerable and shorter. This the Holy Scripture plainly evidences in several places: Matt. 5:22; Matt. 10:15; Matt. 11:21-22; Luke 10:12; Luke 10:14; Luke 41:47-48; Wis. 6:5–8.

All punishments inflicted on the creatures for their sin, or whereby their sin is as it were rewarded, both in this, and in the next world, are comprehended in this one word, Death, as the

---

146 John 3:36

Scripture says, the wages of sin is death.[147]

By this we may see the truth of the divine threatening, and how precisely it was fulfilled, and is daily fulfilled before our eyes, when God threatened our first parents, that in the self-same day, that they should eat of the forbidden fruit, they should surely die.[148] For, from the moment they sinned, they incurred God's wrath and displeasure, lost the Divine image, got an evil conscience, which put them in fear, anxiety and terror; and, in short, they brought upon themselves all sorts of spiritual and bodily plagues and torments. All this is called, in the language of the Holy Ghost, death, and is the wages of sin, or that wherewith sin pays those, who like soldiers, serve and obey it.

> *"Whosoever committeth sin, is the servant of sin."*[149]
> *(John 8:34)*

So that if we take the word death in its most extensive and complete sense, the beginning of it is not only when we die bodily, and our souls are separated from their bodies; but it had its beginning with all men, in the very moment when sin entered into our nature; because death is as naturally in sin, as pain is in sickness.

> *"By one man sin entered into the world, and death by sin; and so death passed upon all men, for all have sinned."*[150] *(Rom. 5:12)*

Wherefore the Holy Scripture speaks very emphatically of such men as are converted to God in this time of grace, that they have passed from death unto life.[151]

---

147 Rom. 6:23
148 Gen. 2:17 compared with Gen. 3:6–10, etc.
149 John 8:34
150 Rom. 5:12
151 John 5:24

> *"And you hath he quickened who were dead in*
> *trespasses and sins."[152] (Eph. 2:1)*

Consequently, they must have been really in death before their conversion, when they were the servants of sin.

> *"For to be carnally minded is death; but to be*
> *spiritually minded is life and peace."[153] (Rom. 8:6)*

Now as death has begun in man with sin, so the more sin increases in man, the more the power and violence of death increases also, in the same manner as the pain and corruption of the body increaseth with the sickness.

> *"For when we were in the flesh, the motions of sin*
> *which were by the law did work in our members to*
> *bring forth fruit unto death."[154] (Rom. 7:5)*

And if men take sin with them out of this world into the next, they likewise carry death with them. If they come to the highest degree of sin and wickedness (which in the Scripture is called the blasphemy against the Holy Ghost, and the sin unto death)[155], and thereby take upon themselves the perfect resemblance of the devil, who seduced them to sin, then they will be banished with him into the outermost regions of darkness and death; that is, precipitated into the lowest hell, or the lake burning with fire and brimstone.[156]

If I was to give a general and scriptural description of death, which is the wages of sin, that is, of all that which the Holy Ghost means by death, both in this and the other world, it would

---

152 Eph. 2:1. See also Eph. 2:5, and Col. 2:13

153 Rom. 8:6

154 Rom. 7:5

155 See Matt. 12:31-32; Mark 3:28-29; Luke 12:10; 1 John 5:16

156 Matt. 8:12; Matt. 22:13; Matt. 25:30; Deut. 32:22 compared with Rev. 20:10; Rev. 20:15; Rev. 21:8

be as follows: "Death, as the wages of sin, is nothing else but the miserable and wretched condition of creatures lying under the dominion of sin, and consequently under the wrath of God, eating of the fruit of their own way,[157] and of the flesh, to which they sowed, reaping corruption,[158] that is, feeling and experiencing through God's just judgment, both in this and the next world, all sorts of spiritual and bodily plagues, flowing quite naturally from their sin and wickedness, and being in proportion and according to the nature thereof; in order that they may be thus convinced, how bad and abominable that is which they have chosen for themselves against the will of God; and so at last, to the everlasting praise and glory of God's justice and mercy, made by these rough and severe means truly subject to God the Father of all spirits, and to his most beloved and only begotten Son Jesus Christ, whom he has appointed Lord over all things, both in this age, and which is to come."[159]

This description takes in all the different kinds of death which divines generally distinguish by bodily, spiritual, and eternal death; since the painful separation of soul and body, with all foregoing bodily afflictions (which is usually called natural death) then the want and loss of the divine image and the grace of God (being called the spiritual death) and lastly, the woeful condition of the damned in hell, either in soul alone, or both in soul and body (which generally goes by the name of eternal death) are in a manner but parts of death, if we take the word in its completest sense.

Concerning the bodily or natural death in particular, whereby the soul and body of man are separated, it may be justly called according to Scripture, first, with respect to believers, a passage

---

157 Prov. 1:31
158 Gal. 6:8
159 See 1 Cor. 15:25; 1 Cor. 15:28 compared with Psalm 145:8–10; Psalm 150:6; Rev. 5:13; Eph. 1:20–22; Phil. 2:9–11; Heb. 2:8

from death into the true eternal life, a putting off all mortality, or a perfect deliverance from the body of death, which in this world they were obliged to bear, and carry about them as a heavy burden. And in this view the natural death is so far from being terrible to the righteous, that it is desirable.[160]

But, secondly, with respect to the wicked and unbelievers, we may rightly call it, a passage out of one miserable land of death into another which is much more miserable and terrible.[161]

But the most proper division of death is to distinguish it according to the Scripture, by the first and second death. It is true that we do not find the name of first death in Scripture, but the denomination of second death implies it. For if there is a second death, there must necessarily be a first death, which is antecedent to the second; because, without it, the name of second death would be without any meaning. But as the term second death, is four times mentioned in Scripture,[162] it is certainly used with design, and implies a first death.

Knowing from what has been said above, that death inseparably hangs together with sin, and as naturally follows upon it, as the wages follow any service, and that sin and death are as much connected as pain and sickness; besides, the Holy Scriptures having given us a precise definition of the second death, viz. that it is a lake burning with fire and brimstone,[163] we may easily comprehend what is meant by the first death.

The first death, therefore, is nothing else but that miserable and painful condition both of soul and body, which men are in while they are under the dominion of sin, and at the same time under the wrath of God; which wretched state began the moment they fell into sin, and if they are not redeemed from it in

---

160 See 2 Cor. 5:1–9; Phil. 1:23; Rev. 14:13; Isa. 57:1-2; Wis. 3:1–4
161 See Luke 16:22-23
162 See Rev. 2:11; Rev. 20:6; Rev. 20:14; Rev. 21:8
163 See Rev. 20:14; Rev. 21:8

this present time of grace, it will continue after the separation of body and soul, under many dreadful punishments and torments, and will grow worse and worse, till at the last judgment, they are either delivered from it through the endless mercies of God, being sufficiently humbled, and so found written in the Book of Life.[164] Or, if the Divine Justice finds it adequate to their iniquity, they are from the first death committed to the second, to receive the full measure of the wrath of God burning over them.[165]

This first death, if represented by the figure of a tyrant, has as it were, two chief provinces and regions where it bears sway, and exercises its power, viz., first, the province of this present wicked world, and the time before the separation of the soul and body, where men in this world are under the dominion of sin and the power of death. And secondly, the woeful rendezvous, or place of torment of the impure souls of the deceased, and the time after the separation of soul and body, until the great day of judgment, where men, going out of this world in an unconverted condition, must remain under the wrath of God and in death, not seeing life.

That not only the unhappy state of men after their decease, but also their sinful condition by nature in this world, where they are servants to sin, is a part of death, the Scripture tells us in plain words, calling such a state, darkness and the shadow of death.[166] Yea, representing them as dead who live in sin,[167] and that such who live in sensual pleasure are dead while they live.[168] They are called living because they enjoy as yet a natural life, common with brutes; but they are dead, because they want the spiritual life,[169] which properly distinguishes men from brutes,

---

164 Rev. 20:12; Rev. 20:15; 1 Pet. 3:19 compared with 1 Pet. 4:6; Hos. 13:14
165 Rev. 20:14-15; Rev. 21:8
166 Luke 1:79
167 Luke 15:24; Luke 15:32; Eph. 2:1–5; Col. 2:13; 1 John 3:14
168 1 Tim. 5:6
169 Eph. 4:18

and makes them truly men, that is, creatures in the image of God.

The doleful regions of the first death, into which unbelievers are banished after their dissolution, have many denominations in Holy Scripture. They are, for instance, called:

The lower parts of the earth.[170]

The nether parts of the earth.[171]

The pit wherein is no water.[172]

The grave, or hell and death.[173]

The sides of the pit.[174]

The darkness and deep.[175]

Darkness, where shall be weeping and gnashing of teeth.[176]

Darkness and the shadow of death, where such have rebelled against the words of God, and contemned the counsel of the most High, sit bound in affliction and iron.[177]

The prison.[178]

---

170 Psalm 63:9
171 Ezek. 31:14–18; Ezek. 32:18–32
172 Zech. 9:11
173 Psalm 49:14-15; Hos. 13:14
174 Isa. 14:15 compared with Isa. 14:9 and Isa. 14:19
175 Psalm 88:6 compared with Psalm 71:20
176 Matt. 8:12; Matt. 22:13; Matt. 25:30
177 Psalm 107:10-11
178 1 Pet. 3:19; Isa. 43:7

Hell, or the place of torment, where the souls of the wicked are tormented as in a flame of fire, without being able to come at the least drop of water to quench their thirst, which place is separated from the delightful mansions of the blessed by a great gulf.[179]

To these names may be added that of the abyss or bottomless pit, wherein Satan will be kept prisoner during the blessed thousand years of the reign of our Lord and savior on the earth.[180]

All which different names and denominations, show plainly enough that the woeful regions of the first death must contain several prisons; and in a certain place of Scripture, they are expressly divided into three headquarters, viz. the Sea, Death (so called in a particular manner), and Hell.[181]

And the difference of these places of confinement designed for the wicked after their departure out of the world (one being doubtless worse than the other) is grounded on the different degrees of their iniquity, where every convict will be ordered by the righteous Judge of all flesh to a prison of death proportional to his crime. This is exemplified to us in the conduct of worldly magistrates, by their not committing all prisoners to the same place of confinement, but every one to a gaol, or part thereof, suitable to his offense.

The second death, following the first, is that most wretched, most woeful, and most unhappy condition of evil men and angels lying under the dominion of sin and the wrath of God, in the fiery lake, whom no foregoing judgments have been able to tame, and who therefore, according to their last doom, must receive the full measure of their well deserved punishments, be absolutely excluded from all the grace and mercy of God, during that very long and terrible age wherein the anger of the Most

179 See Luke 16:23–28
180 Rev. 20:2–3; Rev. 20:7
181 Rev. 20:13

High is to burn against them.[182]

They shall be as unclean dogs cast out of the palace of the King of Heaven, and entirely forsaken of God, and banished from his presence into the most dreadful pain and punishment.[183]

So great will be God's wrath upon those who shall be sentenced to the second death, that even the saints of the Lord will not be permitted to intercede for them, not until they have felt the wrath of God in its highest degree; whereof we have instances in some wicked and obdurate men in this world.[184]

Though not all men, dying in an unsanctified condition of soul, and who are after their decease sentenced to the prisons of the first death, will become a prey to the second death, but some, and without doubt such as are not wicked to the same high degree, nor have had the same means of grace towards their salvation here on earth, as others, will be, through the endless mercies of God preserved from it, as the Holy Scripture plainly shows, after having received a sufficient number of stripes for their sins, and being under such punishment cleansed by the power of the blood of Jesus Christ, which even penetrates into the pit wherein is no water; yet all those that get into the prisons of the first death, will be greatly tormented through fear of the second death; in the same manner as all confined malefactors who deserve to die, must always be in expectation of the punishment of death, though some of them, in consideration of certain circumstances, and through powerful intercession, may not suffer death, but be sentenced to a more tolerable punishment.

That some whose names were not written in the book of life at our Lord's second coming, shall yet be preserved from being cut into the lake of fire, or the second death, is evident from this,

<hr>

182 See Rev. 14:20; Rev. 20:14-15; Rev. 21:8; Rev. 4:10-11; Matt. 3:13; Rev. 25:41; Rev. 25:46; Isa. 33:33

183 See Rev. 22:15; Matt. 8:12; Matt. 25:30; Matt. 24:51; Prov. 1:24–32; Isa. 65:13-14; 2 Thess. 1:9

184 See 1 John 5:16 compared with Jer. 7:16; Jer. 11:14; Jer. 14:11

that the book of life shall be opened, after the second resurrection at the general judgment, and many shall be found written therein, and shall be saved from the second death, who were not worthy of a part in the first resurrection, nor of reigning with Christ.[185]

But the being entirely free from all tormenting fear of the second death, is a peculiar privilege of the faithful conquerors, who during their lifetime here on earth hare been united to Christ, and have suffered him continually to destroy in them the dominion of the devil and sin.

> "He that overcometh shall not be hurt of the second death."[186] (Rev. 2:11)

> "Blessed and holy is he that hath part in the first resurrection; on such the second death hath no power, but they shall be priests of God and of Christ, and shall reign with him a thousand years." [187] (Rev. 20:6)

Such, dying in the Lord are henceforth blessed, come into no judgment, and therefore into no prison of the first death in the next world, and, consequently cannot be hurt by the second death (when even the thoughts thereof are a torment to the prisoners of the first death); for they are perfectly passed from death unto life.[188] When, in the judgment of men, they are said to die, they themselves die not, but it is death which quite dies in and on them, namely, the body of death, to whom they wish no better than entire destruction.

From this we may see that the unhappy state of men leaving this world in unbelief, which we commonly express by the word

185 See Rev. 20:12; Rev. 20:15; 1 Cor. 3:15; Luke 12:47-48
186 Rev. 2:11
187 Rev. 20:6
188 See Rev. 14:13; John 5:24; Rev. 8:61

hell, or damnation, implies much; namely, as Christ says of his Father's house, the dwelling place of the blessed dead, which is generally called heaven, that therein are many mansions;[189] so it is with the habitation of Satan and all unclean spirits in the other world, or the abode of unhappy deceased men; there is not only one, but several gaols and prisons, where every man dying in wickedness will be sent to a prison adapted to his degree of iniquity, there to continue so long, till, according to the true saying of our savior, he has paid all that is due, even to the uttermost farthing, or the very last mite.[190] That is, until he has suffered his due punishment, which is to extend itself to every idle word.[191] And this is the meaning of the words, "He that believeth not shall be damned"[192]; that is, he shall be condemned by the divine justice of God (which is grounded on his eternal love) to such a punishment in the next world, as is adequate to the measure of his iniquity of which he would not suffer himself to be freed in this time of grace.

We may very well express by the words heaven and hell, if taken in their full latitude, the happy and unhappy state of men deceased, either in faith or unbelief; and need not superstitiously interpose a purgatory, since the ultimate end of all punishments, which God (who is love, and whose anger is grounded on love) inflicts on the apostate creatures, both in this and the next world, is, to bring them at last to such a pass, that by the power of the blood of Jesus Christ, shed for the reconciliation of the whole world, sin may be destroyed, and purged out of them. In which sense, all punishments of God, both here and in the other world, may be called purgatories, and we have no reason to look for purgatory only in the world to come; we may find enough of it

---

189 See John 14:2
190 Matt. 18:34; Matt. 5:26; Luke 12:59
191 Matt. 12:36
192 Mark 16:16

in this present world, under all sorts of punishments and afflictions.

But if we will not be made good in this gentle purgatory here, then God, who has bestowed so much on his creatures, and therefore cannot let them be irrecoverably lost, must necessarily after our decease, cast us into one which will burn to the lowest hell, and be able to tame and soften the most wicked wretches, if they were even as bad as the devil himself. God will hold it out with them; let them try if they will not believe it. But may the Lord, through his infinite love, preserve all those that will take warning, from such hardness of heart; and grant that we may much rather choose the afflictions of this life, and the reproach of Christ for our purgatory, which are temporal and light, and will procure for us a far more exceeding and eternal weight of glory;[193] from which all others that must be drawn to God by the judgments of the next world alone will be forever excluded; although, to the praise of God's endless mercy, they will obtain some grace, after they have been sufficiently humbled.

---

193 2 Cor. 4:17

X.

OF THE DIFFERENT DECREES OF ETERNAL GLORY; OR OF THE FIRST BIRTH, AND AFTER BIRTH TO SALVATION.

AS there are many degrees of damnation and unhappiness in the other world, so there are also many degrees of happiness and glory.[194]

The several degrees of happiness in the other world do not only consist, as is most commonly thought, in the difference of the heavenly and divine brightness in which the glorified bodies of the blessed will hereafter shine; but they go much farther, as shall be shown immediately.

The difference of glory in the next world consists chiefly in the first birth, and after birth unto salvation. And consequently there are first born, and after born in the state of salvation.

The first-born unto salvation, to whom belongs the heavenly birth-right, are no other than such men, among the fallen creatures (who must be regenerated and created anew, if they would come again to God) who suffer themselves to be regenerated first, and, through faith, to be united with Christ here in this time of grace, so called in the properest sense.

These are therefore called in Scripture: The Church of the first-born, who are written in heaven;[195] The first fruits of God's creatures;[196] Such as have the first fruits of the Spirit;[197] besides many more glorious names which they have to show their pre-eminence above all the rest of mankind, who will at last be saved

---

194 1 Cor. 15:23-24; 1 Cor. 15:39–42; Psalm 45:14-15; Songs 6:8-9
195 Heb. 12:23
196 James 1:18
197 Rom. 8:23

too by our Universal Redeemer. They are, for instance, called: The Bride of Christ;[198] The friends of Christ;[199] They are called his mother and his brethren;[200] His brethren;[201] The spirits of just men made perfect.[202]

But the Scripture speaks also of a difference between these first-born unto salvation, dividing them, especially in Rev. 11:18, into three classes; viz. the servants of God, or the prophets; the saints; and those that fear the name of the Lord; and these last are again subdivided into small and great. This difference is doubtless grounded, partly, on the different degrees of sanctification to which they attain here; and partly, on the different measure of the spiritual gifts of grace wherewith they are adorned and favored by God, through Jesus Christ.[203]

These first-born and first-fruits are represented as being sealed to the day of redemption, sealed with the Holy Spirit of promise;[204] There is a mark set upon them;[205] They are sealed with the seal of God in their forehead;[206] The name of God is written upon their foreheads;[207] Having this seal, the Lord knoweth them that are his.[208]

It is to these first-born alone, that the promises of the celestial kingdom and priesthood in the future age belong,[209] together with all the unspeakable prerogatives and glories which our Lord and savior has promised to those who are convened to him on earth, love him with all their hearts, and are his constant follow-

---

198 Psalm 45:9–11; Songs 4:8-9; Songs 4:11; Songs 5:1; John 3:29; Rev. 19:7; Rev. 22:17
199 John 15:14-15
200 Matt. 12:49-50; Mark 3:34-35; Luke 8:21
201 Matt. 25:40; Matt. 28:10; Rom. 8:29; Heb. 2:11-12; Heb. 2:17
202 Heb. 12:23
203 See Rom. 12:3–8; 1 Cor. 12:4–31
204 Eph. 1:13-14; Eph. 4:30
205 See Ezek. 4:4
206 Rev. 7:2–8
207 Rev. 14:1; Rev. 3:20; Rev. 22:4
208 2 Tim. 2:19
209 See Matt. 25:34; Rev. 5:10; Rev. 20:4–6; Rev. 22:5

ers, whereof, especially the book of the Revelations is full.[210]

This was represented in the Old Testament by the first-born children of the holy patriarchs, who by virtue of their birth-right were entitled to the sovereignty or dominion, as also to the priesthood over the rest of their brethren, and the whole family.[211]

In the place of the first-born, God afterward adopted the Levites among the children of Israel; and the whole tribe of Levi, instead of the first-born, were entrusted with the oracles of God, and invested with the sacerdotal office, as the government of state or royalty was transferred to the tribe of Judah.[212]

And we find that the high prerogative of the spiritual birth-right was even prefigured in the Old Testament in general, by all the first-born and first-fruits, both of clean beasts, and of the fruits of the earth, which God would have sanctified unto him in a special manner, as appears by many places in the Pentateuch.[213] The first born to salvation are those few who in their lifetime find the narrow way to eternal life, and penetrate through the straight gate; whereas such as go the broad way of the flesh, leading to perdition, are many, yea, the greatest number.[214] The first-born are the few elect compared with the many who are called, but on the account of their unbelief and disobedience are rejected.[215] These, after the sad example of Esau (who for one morsel of meat sold his birth-right) are deprived of the enjoyment of the inexpressible privileges and glories of the heavenly birthright.[216]

---

210 See Rev. 2:7; Rev. 2:10-11; Rev. 2:17; Rev. 2:26–28; Rev. 3:5; Rev. 3:12; Rev. 3:20-21; Rev. 21:7; Rev. 22:3–5; Rev. 22:14

211 Gen. 49:8 compared with Gen. 14:31-34; Gen. 27:19; Gen 27:28-29; Gen. 27:33–40

212 Numb. 3:12; Numb. 3:40–51; Numb. 8:5–26; Gen. 49:8–10; 1 Chron. 5:1-2

213 Exod. 8:2; Exod. 8:12–16; Exod. 22:29; Exod. 22:30; Exod. 23:19; Exod. 24:19-20; Exod. 24:26; Lev. 27:36; Numb. 3:13; Numb. 8:16-17. See Luke 2:22–24; Rom. 11:16

214 Matt. 7:13-14; Luke 13:24

215 Matt. 22:14; Luke 19:24

216 Heb. 12:16-17 compared with Gen. 25:33-34; Gen. 27:33–38

By the after-born to salvation, are chiefly meant all the rest of mankind, who in their life-time neglect repentance, and the purification of their souls, selling like Esau, their birth-right for a mess of pottage of lentils; that is, giving it in exchange for the vanities of this world, and must therefore, after their departure hence, remain under God's wrath, and by the long-lasting and terrible judgments of the next world be humbled and made fit for the participation of some enjoyment of the endless mercies of God, through Christ the universal savior and Reconciler of all fallen creatures, and thus, in their way be regenerated unto life, after the already glorified first-born children of God. To the afterborn belong too, as a supplement, the fallen angels, as we have shown above.

Although the phrase, after-born to salvation, is not to be literally met with in the Bible, yet the thing itself is grounded therein. For, if it be true, that at the last judgment many of the dead that are given up by the sea, death, and hell, as prisons of the first death, will be found written in the book of life,[217] and shall be delivered from the full power of the second death (between whom and the first-born, that have part in the first resurrection, and are to reign with Christ during the blessed thousand years, or the day of his glorious marriage, the Scriptures expressly distinguishes);[218] yea if it be true, that at last will follow a Universal Restoration of all apostatized creatures through a general subjection, solemnly promised in Scripture,[219] then it must be true too, that all these together may be justly called after-born unto salvation, because they are not of the number of the first-born, but will, a long time after the glorification of these, be made truly subject unto God, and Christ, and in their way be born again unto life eternal.

217 See Rev. 20:12-13; Rev. 20:15 compared with 1 Pet. 3:19-20; 1 Pet. 4:6
218 See Rev. 20:5 compared with Rev. 20:12; Rev. 20:18
219 1 Cor. 15:24–28; Phil. 2:10-11; Rev. 5:13

Now, of these after-born to salvation there are chiefly two sorts. For some are afterborn out of the first death; and others after-born out of the second death.

The after-born out of the first death are, as aforesaid, those deceased, who, after the blessed thousand years of Christ's marriage, at the last judgment, will be given up by the sea, death, and hell, and be found written in the book of life.[220] And so through the endless mercy of God be saved from the second death and from its full power over them; though the ideas of it will have been great torment to them in the prisons of the first death.

The forerunners of these after-born were the spirits unto whom Christ, at his descent into hell, preached the Gospel of their Redemption.[221]

The after-born out of the second death, are all the rest of mankind, and the fallen angels, who, under all the foregoing dreadful judgments of the first death, will continue in their wickedness, and therefore must be humbled in the fiery lake, by the most horrible and consummate judgments of the second death, and be brought at last to bow every one of their knees before Christ, and so have their share too in the eternal redemption obtained by him for us.[222]

That there may be a difference again between these after-born out of the second death, as to the time of their restoration, seems very probable by what is said.[223] For in the first place it is said of some that are cast into the fiery lake, that with the devil they shall be tormented therein forever, and ever; but in the other two places, which likewise speak of such as will be cast into the lake burning with fire and brimstone, we do not find this addition,

---

220 See Rev. 20:15 compared with Hos. 13:14, and Zech. 9:11

221 1 Pet. 3:19-20; 1 Pet. 4:6; Psalm 68:18; Eph. 4:8–10; Col. 2:15

222 Phil. 2:10-11; Rev. 5:13; Heb. 9:12

223 Rev. 20:10 compared with Rev. 20:15; as also Rev. 21:8

but it is only said that they are cast into the lake of fire, and that they shall have their part therein.

This has, without doubt, a particular signification, since the Holy Ghost in the Scriptures neither inserts nor omits anything without design.

The very last of all that will be restored are the blasphemers against the Holy Ghost, and the seducers of the whole race of men, to wit, Lucifer and his angels.[224] These will be obliged to remain prisoners under the divine wrath, without remission of sins, during the whole eternity or age of Christ's reign with his people in the world to come, and through God's just judgments, shall not be restored until that point of time, or just before it, when the future age or world is to be changed into that still or silent eternity, wherein God is to be all in all, after Jesus Christ shall have subdued every thing to himself, and brought all into order and harmony.[225]

Although these after-born to salvation, who, in due season, by Christ, the universal savior, will be delivered both from the first and second death, will also, after such redemption, receive a blessing with Esau,[226] and will partake of some beatitude, which the Scripture describes in this manner: In the name of Jesus they shall bow their knees, etc.[227]; Shall be subdued unto Christ, and thus become the subjects of God;[228] and shall praise God and the Lamb;[229] yet they will be excluded to all endless eternity, from all the before-mentioned glories, peculiar to the first-born, namely, from the reigning with Christ, and the celestial priest-hood, both during the aforesaid blessed thousand years, and all the succeeding ages of ages: and thus, in some measure, they will undergo

---

224 Matt. 12:31-32; Mark 3:28-29; Luke 12:10; Rev. 20:10 compared with Rev. 11:15; Rev. 22:5
225 1 Cor. 15:28
226 See Heb. 11:20 compared with Gen. 27:34–40
227 Phil. 2:10-11
228 1 Cor. 15:28
229 Rev. 5:13

an absolutely endless punishment; that is, they will suffer *pœ-nam damni*, or sustain the loss of the quite particular prerogative annexed to the spiritual birth-right, as Esau lost his birth-right.[230] However, so, that at last, having sufficiently regretted their irreparable loss, they will be very well content with that share of salvation which the infinite grace of God, for the sake of Jesus Christ, our universal Redeemer, will give them, and will rejoice at the far more exceeding and eternal weight of glory, which the first-born shall receive, and will humble themselves to the utmost before them and their glorious head, Jesus Christ.[231]

Now this entire deprivation of the birth-right, together with all the inexpressible pains which they shall have suffered for their sins, both in the first and second death, will be punishment enough for them; from which eternal damnation most graciously keep us, good Lord God.

---

230 Heb. 12:16-17
231 Rev. 3:9

XI.

WHAT THE SCRIPTURE MEANETH BY THIS PRESENT WORLD, THE WORLD TO COME, AND THE STILL OR SILENT ETERNITY.

THE Holy Scripture in many places speaks of this, or the present world.[232] In some passages the world to come is mentioned.[233] And once at least, the still eternity, which God inhabiteth is named:

> "Thus saith the High and lofty One, that inhabiteth
> eternity, whose name is Holy, I dwell in the high and
> holy place," etc.[234] (Isa. 57:15)

And some think there is an intimation of the stillness or quietness of that eternity in Isa. 32:17-18.

By this world, the Scriptures in general mean nothing else but this present *aiona*, or period of time, which in so far as it is called the wicked world, had its beginning with the apostasy of the creatures, especially the fall of our first parents, whereby sin and death were introduced into the world; and will last until the coming of Christ, when he will judge the anti-christian race of men, and consume and destroy Antichrist with the spirit of his mouth, and the brightness of his coming.[235] In this period of time, that which is evil always had the sway over that which is good,

---

232 See Matt. 12:32; Matt. 13:22; Matt. 13:39-40; Matt. 13:49; Matt. 24:3; Mark 4:19; Luke 16:8; Luke 20:34; Rom. 12:2; 1 Cor. 1:20; 1 Cor. 2:6-7; 1 Cor. 3:18; 2 Cor. 4:4; Gal. 1:4; Eph. 1:21; Eph. 6:12; 1 Tim. 6:17; 1 Tim. 4:10; Tit. 2:12

233 Matt. 12:32; Mark 10:30; Luke 18:30; Luke 20:35; Eph. 1:21; Heb. 6:5

234 Isa. 57:15

235 See Dan. 7:26-27; 2 Thess. 2:8 compared with Rev. 14:11; Rev. 14:20-21; Matt. 13:39–42

and will have it to the coming of Christ,[236] so that we must not expect constantly better times, but rather that things will grow worse and worse the nearer the coming of the Lord approaches.[237] Howbeit I will not deny, but that before the end of this wicked world, or age, there may be made a good beginning and preparation towards a downright reformation in the church of God, through the power of the gospel of the kingdom, which may be preached throughout the whole world (though under many tribulations and persecutions); for which indeed the words of our savior,[238] afford us good hopes.

But this is certain, that there will not be a thorough reformation before the coming of the Son of Man; and the reason of it is that the devil is the prince or god of this world, or age,[239] and consequently, worketh in the children of disobedience,[240] who always were the most numerous in the world, and will be so until the day of the coming of the Lord; but then, and not before, the power of the devil, and the anti-christian kingdom of the beast and the false prophet, will have an end, according to the plain testimonies of Scripture.[241]

This *aion*, or period of time, is again subdivided by the Holy Scripture into two special periods, or worlds: viz. into the wicked world before the flood, or into the old world,[242] and into the present wicked world,[243] or the age of the world after the flood, under the four empires, represented by the four beasts in Daniel's prophecy, which began soon after the deluge, and will, as aforesaid, end at the coming of Christ.[244]

---

236 See Rev. 13:6–8, etc.
237 Matt. 24:37–39; Luke 17:26–30; Luke 18:8; 1 Thess. 5:2-3; 2 Tim. 3:1–5; 2 Tim. 3:13; Rev. 3:10; Rev. 6:11; Rev. 12:12.
238 Matt. 24:14; Mark 13:10
239 See John 14:30; Luke 4:6; 2 Cor. 4:4; Eph. 6:12
240 Eph. 2:2
241 2 Thess. 2:8; Rev. 14:20-21
242 2 Pet. 2:5; 2 Pet. 3:6
243 Gal. 1:4
244 See Dan. 2:31-45; Dan. 7 wholly.

By the world to come, the Holy Scripture does not mean properly and absolutely an endless eternity, but those *aionas*, or long lasting periods of time, which although they exist already, with respect to Christ and his saints, received by him into glory, yet the full manifestation thereof is to succeed the period of this present wicked world, and will only begin with the coming of Christ, and the commencement of his glorious kingdom, [245] and will reach to that point of time when both the first and second death will be entirely abolished, and the Son of God, after all things have been put in subjection under him (nothing excepted, but his heavenly Father) shall deliver up the kingdom, or the whole restored creation (which shall until then be under his government) to God his Father, and himself be subject unto him who put all things under him, that God may be all in all. [246]

In all these periods of time, the Good, namely, Christ, with his first born brethren, as kings and priests, will forever and without interruption, rule over the bad, as his and their enemies, and effect the entire restoration of all things; that is, he will subdue and reconcile all things unto himself and his heavenly Father, and bring them into that harmony and order, wherein every thing was created in the beginning. [247]

Now, to those periods of time of the holy and righteous world to come, and its manifestation, belong, first, the thousand years of Christ's marriage day; the age commonly called the Millennium or Sabbath of Rest, when Satan shall be bound and confined in the bottomless pit for a thousand years, the first resurrection shall take place, and the first born saints shall reign with Christ on the earth a thousand years. [248]

Also, secondly, to the next world, particularly belong all the

---

245 Rev. 1:15–18; Rev. 12:10 compared with Dan. 7:14; Dan. 7:26-27

246 Heb. 2:8; 1 Cor. 15:24–28

247 See Rev. 15:15; Rev. 5:10; Rev. 22:5; Dan. 7:18; Dan. 7:27; 1 Cor. 15:28; Phil. 2:10-11; Col. 1:20; Acts 3:21; Gen. 1:31

248 See Rev. 20:1–6; compared with Rev. 5:10, and Rev. 2:26-27; Rev. 3:21

other *aionos ton aionon*, or many long lasting periods of time, which are to succeed the above mentioned thousand years; during which periods all things will be subdued and restored, and at the close of which, Christ will resign the kingdom to the Father, that God may be all in all.

By the still or absolutely endless eternity, wherein God dwelleth, is meant in Holy Scripture, that eternal and endless duration of the uncreated and Divine Being, and the most perfect and invariable beatitude which he possesses. Which, with respect to God, has been without beginning, from all inconceivable eternity, and still is going through all created eternities both of this and the next world, and is their very source and principle, but with respect to the creatures, it will not manifest itself in the most perfect manner, till at that point of the created eternities, when Christ after the entire restoration of all things, will give up the kingdom to his heavenly Father, and be subject to him who put all things under him, that God may be all in all. In this still eternity which will then be manifested to the creatures, and which will, as it were, swallow up the future world, and wherein God is to reign in that true order as is most agreeable to him, there will be no more sensible knowledge nor hearing of that which is called Devil, Sin, Death, Wrath, or Hell, than there was when all creatures were yet hid in the eternal creating power of the everlasting God, or when in the beginning of the creation, they were yet altogether very good. Because every thing that is diabolical, namely, sin and the first and second death following it, will in the most consummate manner be destroyed, and swallowed up in victory, and the whole creation shall be most perfectly delivered from all evil; and the kingdom, power, and glory shall be given to him to whom it belongs for ever and ever.[249] Amen.

---

[249] See Isa. 57:15; 1 Cor. 15:24–28; 1 Cor. 15:54–56 compared with 1 Cor 15:26. See also Rom. 8:19–23 compared with Gen. 1:31; Job 38:7; Rev. 21:1–5; Matt. 6:13

The divine subjection of the Son of God, following upon the next world, and belonging to the still eternity, will by no means lessen the glory of Christ and his saints, but will rather be an occasion of something much more excellent and glorious than his former blessed reign, during the thousand years, and in the succeeding eternities of eternities. For as long as these ages last, so long will sin, or at least imperfection, be in many creatures; which at this time will not be fit in general to be ruled immediately by God, and therefore must be governed by mediators. But when the Son of God shall deliver up the kingdom to the Father, and himself be subject to him that put all things under him, then will neither sin nor imperfection any more be found in any of God's creatures; but they will be as immediately governed by God himself, as the humanity of Jesus Christ is governed by the Godhead, everyone according to his nature; and therefore there will be no farther need of government by the mediatorial economy, the design whereof had been merely that all things might be subdued unto Christ, and under him to God.[250] Now, when this design shall be completely obtained, then will also cease the means ordered for obtaining it; namely, the particular sort of government of Christ and his saints, during the thousand years, and the ages of ages following; but the glory of Christ and of his saints in the future universal subjection in the still eternity, will be without end.

Whosoever rightly looks into, and well understands this mystery of the difference between this world, the next world, and the still, or absolutely endless eternity, to him the center of the Holy Scripture, and of all the prophecies contained therein are open; because they are partly fulfilled in this world, partly in the future world, and all the rest will be accomplished in the still eternity, in so far as there is a difference between it and the world to

---

250 1 Cor. 15:24-25, etc.; Phil. 2:10-11

come.

From this principle we may also very easily and with the greatest importance answer the objection that is made against the general restoration, from Matt. 12:31-32. It is indeed true, that all manner of sin and blasphemy shall be forgiven unto men, except the blasphemy against the Holy Ghost; those who are guilty of that sin shall have no forgiveness neither in this world or age, nor in the world or age to come, but are in danger of eternal damnation, according to Mark 3:29.

By the world or age to come, in the first mentioned place, without doubt is meant the whole time from the beginning of the Millennium to the last judgment. For within this time not only many millions will be converted to God, and receive forgiveness of their sins, but also many of those that have been lying in the sea, in death, and in hell, as miserable prisoners of the first death, will at last, at the opening of the books of judgment, be found written in the book of life, and thus obtain remission of their sins, and be delivered from the full power of the second death.[251]

But the blasphemers against the Holy Ghost, and all such who have committed the sin unto death, for whom we are commanded not to pray;[252] and such who have sinned willfully after having received the knowledge of the truth;[253] such who have crucified to themselves the Son of God afresh, and put him to an open shame;[254] the professed enemies of Christ and his believers, and among those particularly the blaspheming beast, and false prophet, who in this world have so long and continually been afflicting and persecuting Christ and his followers, will then, in virtue of God's most holy justice, be treated in the very same

---

251 See Rev. 20:12-13; Rev. 20:15 compared with Hos. 13:14; Zech. 9:11; 1 Cor. 3:15
252 1 John 5:16
253 Heb. 10:26–29
254 Heb. 6:6

manner as they have treated the servants of Christ here: they will be rejected, esteemed accursed, and will be cast into the lake of fire and brimstone, which is the second death, partly before and partly after the thousand years, without any grace or mercy; and consequently will obtain no forgiveness of their sins, but be obliged to suffer what their deeds deserve, as the Scripture plainly testifies.[255]

But it does by no means follow from hence that these sinners can never be cleansed from their sins, and made truly subject unto Christ and God, before or at the expiration of those ages of ages which shall succeed the thousand years, or the age to come, when such sinners, together with all other rebellious creatures, shall have been sufficiently punished for their wickedness in the burning lake. Then, instead of contradicting Christ in a presumptuous manner, as they did not only in this world, but even in the day of judgment,[256] they shall most humbly bow their knees before him, and become heartily subject unto him, and through him be reconciled unto God.[257]

---

255 See Matt. 25:41; Matt. 25:46; Rev. 19:20; Rev. 20:15; Rev. 21:8; Rev. 14:9–11
256 See Matt. 25:44; Matt. 7:22
257 See Phil. 2:10-11; 1 Cor. 15:24–28; Col. 1:20

XII.

CONTAINING THE CLEAREST SENTENCES OF THE HOLY SCRIPTURES WHICH TREAT OF THE GENERAL RESTORATION OF ALL MEN AND CORRUPT CREATURES.

As the center of the whole Bible, where at?? all its contents aim is this, that in the beginning God created every thing very good; and that by Christ, who is the wisdom and power of God, by whom all things were made at first, all whatsoever is corrupted through sin, must at last be made good again: so may anyone whose eyes are opened to see clearly into this point, find a great many testimonies of this eternal truth both in the books of the Old and New Testament. But we will for our present purpose, only allege some of the plainest sentences.

First, some very plain texts of Scripture, treating of the final restoration of all corrupt men:

> "Therefore, as by the offense of one, judgment came
> upon all men to condemnation; even so by the
> righteousness of one, the free gift came upon all men
> unto justification of life. For as by one man's
> disobedience, many were made (or represented)
> sinners; so by the obedience of one shall (the same)
> many be made (or represented) righteous. Moreover,
> the law entered that the offense might abound: but
> where sin, abounded, Grace did much more abound:
> That, as sin hath reigned unto death, even so might
> grace reign through righteousness unto eternal life by

Jesus Christ our Lord.[258] *(Rom. 5:18-21)*

"For God hath concluded them all (or shut them up together) in unbelief, that he might have mercy upon all."[259] *(Rom. 11:32)*

"For as in Adam all die, even so in Christ shall all be made alive. But every man in his own (or in his particular) order."[260] *(1 Cor. 4:22-23)*

These texts of Scripture most evidently show and foretell us, that as really as sin and condemnation came upon and entered into all men, even so really and certainly will righteousness and life come again into all corrupt men by Jesus Christ, even that true life of God, which alone is the real life of men; and that they shall at last altogether actually enjoy the mercy of God as truly and really as they have felt the power of sin, and have been concluded under unbelief. In short, that as sin hath reigned in and unto death, even so shall grace reign through righteousness unto eternal life, by Jesus Christ our Lord. Now, sin hath reigned in such a manner, that it has actually made all men its subjects, and brought death upon them; therefore, without contradiction, grace must also reign in such a manner as to bring all men again to its obedience, and consequently restore in them righteousness and eternal life. And, indeed, so much the more, because it is expressly said, that grace is not only to abound as much as sin, but even to abound much more than sin.

But how can grace be said to abound much more than sin, if, according to the common hypothesis we avow on the one hand, that it is able to justify and save all men, but on the other hand

---

258 Rom. 5:18-21
259 Rom. 11:32
260 1 Cor. 4:22-23

deny that it will actually justify and save all men? For sin was not only able to make all men unrighteous, and to bring death upon them, but it has actually made them all in general unrighteous, and brought death upon them.

> "We trust in the living God, who is the savior (or Restorer) of all men, especially of those that believe."[261] (1 Tim. 4:10)

As really, now, as all true believers are delivered from sin and death by this universal savior, so really and certainly must all the rest of mankind be finally delivered therefrom; since otherwise God would be but a titular and not an actual savior or Restorer of all the rest of men. For it is not only requisite that a savior and Redeemer pay the ransom for the prisoners, but that he also set them actually free from their imprisonment.

> "Now is the judgment of this world; (or, now sentence passeth upon this world, and it is, as it were condemned together with its prince;) now shall the prince of this world be cast out. And I, if I be lifted up from the earth, will draw all men unto me."[262] (John 12:31-32)

Here again it is incontestably shown, that a little before our savior's passion, it had been firmly decreed in heaven by an irrevocable sentence passed upon this world, that the certain fruits and effects of the sufferings and death of Christ should be, that Satan, or the prince of this world, should be entirely divested and cast out of his pretended ungodly sovereignty over mankind; and that, on the contrary, Christ lifted up, or crucified, should at last actually draw all men, who before had been subject to the devil,

---

261 1 Tim. 4:10
262 John 12:31-32

unto himself, and thus of necessity, bring them again into their order and subjection under God.

> "Then said Jesus, Father, forgive them; for they know
> not what they do."[263] (Luke 23:34)

> "Father, I thank thee, that thou hast heard me: and I
> know that thou hearest me always."[264] (John 11:41-42)

In the first of these sentences, Christ prays for the worst of villains under the sun, namely, for his persecutors, and those who crucified him; and consequently for all such too, as have crucified him in his faithful members from the beginning of the world, and those who still persecute and crucify him, and will continue to do so, to the end of this world, or wicked age. Now, his prayer is this, that the heavenly Father will readily forgive their sins, or, that he will once again bring them into the right order of repentance and faith, wherein their sins may be forgiven them. And that this prayer and intercession of Christ, as well as all others which he ever made and does still make, must at last be fully heard and granted, our dear savior once for all assures us in the second sentence, taken from John 11:41-42:

> "Deliver us from evil: for thine is the kingdom, and
> the power, and the glory, forever. Amen."[265] (Matt.
> 6:13)

Among the most evident proofs of the blessed general restoration of all mankind, we may also with very good reason reckon this mysterious prayer of our Lord, especially the last petition of it. For it is indisputably true that the Lord hath obliged us to pray therein, for all men, without any exception. But what

263 Luke 23:34
264 John 11:41-42
265 Matt. 6:13

is it that we are to desire for them? That his name may be sanctified by them; his kingdom come into them; and his will be done
by and through them, etc. but especially, that he may deliver every one of them from evil, that is, actually free them from sin
and the power of the devil, or from all pain and woe following
upon sin, both in this and the next world. In short, that God may,
through Jesus Christ, the universal savior, justify, convert, and
save them. And, indeed, all for this reason; as the conclusion
shows, because the kingdom, or sovereignty over all mankind,
belongs by no means to the devil, but solely to our dear Lord and
God.

He alone has the power, and is able to deliver mankind from
evil. And lastly, because to him alone, and to no other being, belongs, and will be forever attributed, the glory and honor of this
great work, for the execution of which all creatures will bless
and praise him to all eternity.[266]

You will say, it is true enough that in the Lord's prayer, we
pray that God may convert and save all men, without any exception at all, but that does not argue that with respect to all men
this will be really done; because the greatest part of them frustrate on themselves the effect of this prayer, by their own constant impenitence.

But hear, ye that make this objection, pray what then, is the
meaning of the word Amen, which we are obliged to put as a
seal to this most excellent prayer? Is it not as much as to say,
Verily, so be it? And therefore, must not all the petitions of the
Lord's prayer, but especially the last, be certainly granted in favor of every man, as truly and really as the children of God pray
for, and desire the good things expressed therein, according to
his earnest will, and as surely as they cannot pray in vain? And
that we may never doubt of the final accomplishment of the

---

266 See Psalm 114:10-11; Psalm 150:6; Rev. 5:13

united prayers of the saints, our blessed savior has said:

> *"And whatsoever ye shall ask in my name that will I*
> *do, that the Father may be glorified in the Son. If ye*
> *shall ask anything in my name I will do it."*[267] *(John*
> *14:13-14)*

And again:

> *"Verily, verily, I say unto you, Whatsoever ye shall ask*
> *the Father in my name, he will give it you. Hitherto*
> *have ye asked nothing in my name; ask and ye shall*
> *receive, that your joy may be full."*[268] *(John 16:23-24)*

And John says:

> *"And this is the confidence that we have in him, that*
> *if we ask anything according to his will he heareth us.*
> *And if we know that he heareth us, whatsoever we*
> *ask, we know that we have the petitions that we*
> *desired of him."*[269] *(1 John 5:14-15)*

From which infallibly follows, that although many thousands of men hinder the efficacy of this prayer on themselves in this world, and become a prey to the jaws of hell, yet they will not be able to hinder it forever and to all endless eternity. That which is good will at last surely conquer that which is evil. God knows how to make those willing that are at present unwilling to be converted unto him; so that such prodigal sons through his grace will be glad to return to their Father's house, after they have long enough felt the torments and miseries of the fiery lake, if it be never so long before it be brought about.

But if it was an unquestionable truth, as our adversaries pre-

---

267 John 14:13-14
268 John 16:23-24
269 1 John 5:14-15

tend, that most men will remain distant from God, and will frustrate on themselves the granting of this prayer, to all endless eternity, then Christ would have taught us to pray not only wavering or double minded, but even in unbelief and lying, and consequently such a prayer as the Spirit of Christ absolutely rejects and condemns,[270] namely, he would have earnestly commanded us to pray for all men without exception, that God might at last convert and save them, and always to add Amen! to the end that we might by no means doubt but this our prayer of universal love would be heard (which universal love that is to extend itself even to the worst of enemies, and from which this prayer is to flow, our savior inculcates a little before he gives the instruction in the duty of prayer)[271] though nevertheless it was already decreed by God from all eternity, and we were obliged to believe it as a truth, that the greatest part of men, of whom he had foreseen, that during this short lifetime, they would remain in unbelief, and hinder on themselves the efficacy of this prayer, and should therefore not only be greatly punished in the next world (which is true), but that they also should forever and without end remain in the power of sin and the devil, and never be converted.

But, far be it from all believers to impute such a blasphemy to their Redeemer, to have taught them with a feigned faith to pray for things which they think can never be done, and which at the bottom they do not believe. May the Lord rebuke thee, O Satan, for endeavoring to make God's children believe such a calumny against their gracious God and dear Redeemer. Since, therefore, we are commanded to pray for the salvation of all men, without wrath or doubting, and to ask in faith, nothing wavering, we may be assured that it is the absolute will of God that all men

---

270 James 1:6–8 compared with 1 Tim. 2:8
271 See Matt. 5:44–48

shall be saved, and come in the knowledge of the truth.[272]

Note well, to the texts of Scripture which prove the restoration of all fallen men, may very reasonably be reckoned also
those that treat of God's universal love towards all men; of his
earnest will to have them saved in general, and without the least
exception; as also those that speak of universal redemption,
etc.[273]

From these important articles of faith we may certainly infer
the actual restoration of all men; because it is impossible for God
to will anything in vain to all endless eternity; and it is absolutely false, and the utmost derogation of Christ's redemption, to
pretend, that he should have shed his most precious and divine
blood quite in vain, and without the least blessed effect for but
one of his creatures. Not to mention, that God has also most
plainly foretold, that the condition of salvation, namely, righteousness flowing from repentance and faith, onto which salvation is infallibly annexed, shall at last be fulfilled with respect to
all men, who by Adam's sin have become unrighteous, as has
been shown above, from Rom. 5:18–21.

To the arguments for the restoration of fallen men, belong
also with good reason, the places of Scripture that treat either of
a past or future deliverance of some souls out of a middle state of
pain, which is owned by many who oppose the entire and general Restoration.[274] Those who understand the above cited texts,
of a deliverance from a middle state, which they allow of as
aforesaid, while at the same time they deny the entire restoration of all men, out of the fiery lake, must, I say, at least grant us
thus much, that from the redemption out of a middle painful

---

272 See 1 Tim. 2:1–8; James 1:6
273 As for instance, Ezek. 18:23; Ezek. 18:32; Ezek. 33:11; Matt. 18:11; Matt. 18:14; John
   1:29; John 3:16-17; 2 Cor. 5:14-15; 1 Tim. 2:4–6; Heb. 2:8-9; 2 Pet. 2:1; 2 Pet. 3:9; 1
   John 2:2
274 As, 1 Pet. 3:19-20; 1 Pet. 4:6; Eph. 4:8-9; Psalm 68:18; 1 Cor. 3:15; Rev. 20:12-13; Rev.
   20:15 compared with Hos. 13:14; Zech. 9:11; 1 Sam. 2:6; Rev. 1:18

state, we may with, some probability conclude the redemption of such as are cast into the fiery lake, or lowest hell.

But whosoever pondereth that with God there is no respect of persons, will easily conceive, that our conclusion is not only probable, but most true and just. For why should God, who is no respecter of persons, neither in the execution of his justice nor in the display of his mercy, deliver some from a painful condition by Jesus Christ, and not at last others also? It is enough that he punishes some more severely and longer than others, which must be, on account of his most holy justice; because some have sinned more than others.

Secondly, plain texts of Scripture, treating of the final restoration of all corrupt creatures, and consequently not only of men, but likewise of the fallen angels (aiming at least plainly at the latter) who in the beginning were of the number of the principal creatures of God:

> "Jehovah is good to all, and his tender mercies are over all his works."[275] (Psalm 145:9)

> "But thou hast mercy upon all; for thou canst do all things, and winkest at the sins of men, because they should amend. For thou lovest all the things that are, and abhorrest nothing which thou hast made: for never wouldst thou have made anything if thou hadst hated it. And how could anything have endured, if it had not been thy will? or been preserved, if not called by thee? But thou sparest all, for they are thine, O Lord, thou lover of souls. For thine incorruptible Spirit is in all things."[276] (Wis. 11:23-26)

---

275 Psalm 145:9
276 Wis. 11:23–26; Wis. 12:1

"Thou art worthy, O Lord, to receive glory, and honor,
and power: for thou hast created all things, and for
thy pleasure they are, and were created."[277] (Rev. 4:11)

In these passages we are plainly told, that the mercy of God, or his tender love, does not only extend itself to men, but universally towards all creatures, that through the will of God have their being, and stand in need of mercy; and consequently also towards the fallen angels, as far as they are creatures of God; which tender love of God must necessarily at last effect or bring about the restoration of all corrupt creatures, for it is not a weak or faint, but an almighty love.

"Out of him (God) and through him, and into him,
are all things: to him be glory forever. Amen."[278] (Rom.
2:36)

Thus this important text may be very well rendered. Now if all things (to which indisputably belong as well all fallen angels as corrupt men) that are come forth out of God, who is love essentially, or out of his everlasting creating power, and are upheld by him, shall return into the same God of love, or be pervaded and quite swallowed up by his loving spirit, what, then, will become of sin, which separates God and the creature, and the unhappiness hanging together with it; will it not of necessity, by this returning or reflux of the creatures into God (however without destroying the true difference between the being of the Creator and that of the creatures) be lost and entirely abolished?

"For by him (Jesus Christ, the only begotten Son of
God) were all things created that are in heaven, and
that are in earth, visible and invisible, whether they

---

be thrones, or dominions, or principalities, or powers:
all things were created by him and for him. And he is
before all things, and by him all things consist. And
he is the head of the body, the church: who is the
beginning, the first born from the dead; that in all
things he might have the pre-eminence. For it pleased
the Father that in him should all fulness dwell. And
(having made peace through the blood of his cross) by
him to reconcile all things unto himself, by him, I say,
whether they be things in earth, or things in
heaven."[279] *(Col. 1:16-20)*

This passage teaches us the extent of the reconciliation made by Christ, namely, that it extends itself over the whole creation. Therefore, the fallen angels must also necessarily have their share in it, for they do incontestably belong to the invisible things created by Christ, and consequently to all things, or the things in heaven reconciled by him. And though it is true that this reconciliation chiefly concerns corrupt men and angels, that through sin are separated from God, nevertheless all the rest of the creatures partake of and are benefited by it. It affords for instance, matter of much joy to the holy angels, when, by virtue of this reconciliation, the apostatized creatures are convened to God, and thereby anew received into the communion and friendship of these holy spirits.[280] It will also be by the energy of this reconciliation, that in time to come the curse which through sin was brought upon the creation, and has mixed itself with it,[281] will be entirely removed from all the rest of the creatures.

"He (God) hath abounded towards us in all wisdom
and prudence, having made known unto us the

---

279 Col. 1:16-20
280 Luke 15:10; 1 Pet. 1:12; Heb. 12:22
281 Gen. 3:17; Rom. 8:20-22

mystery of his will, according to his good pleasure,
which he hath purposed in himself: that in the
dispensation of the fulness of times, he might gather
together (or rehead) all things in Christ, both which
are in heaven (or, in the heavens) and which are on
earth, even in him."[282] (Eph. 1:8-10)

This is another plain testimony of the blessed restoration of all rebellious creatures (that were corrupted through sin) under Christ their true and lawful head; and by the things in heaven, which are to be gathered together in Christ, or subdued again under him as their chief, no other creatures than the fallen angels can be meant, who also in several other places in the Holy Scriptures are expressly reckoned amongst the things in the heaven,[283] since they were not only formerly celestial creatures, but have even to this day their seat in a certain part of the heavens, viz. in the air; which place they will not lose till just before the blessed millennium, when they will be thrown down from heaven to the earth, from thence into the bottomless pit, and finally into the fiery lake.[284]

"Thou hast put all things under his feet: For in that he
put all in subjection under him, he left nothing that is
not put under him. But now we see not yet all things
put under him."[285] (Heb. 2:8)

"Then cometh the end, when he shall have delivered
up the kingdom to God, even the Father; when he
shall have put down all rule, and all authority, and
power. For he must reign till he hath put all enemies

---

282 Eph. 1:8-10
283 Rev. 12:7; Eph. 6:12; Eph. 2:2
284 See Rev. 12:7–9 compared with Eph. 2:2; Rev. 20:3; Rev. 20:10
285 Heb. 2:8

under his feet. The last enemy that shall be destroyed
is Death. For he hath put all things under his feet: but
when he saith, all things are put under him, it is
manifest that he is excepted who did put all things
under him. And when all things shall be subdued unto
him, then shall the Son of man also himself be subject
unto him that put all things under him, that God may
be all in all."[286] *(1 Cor. 15:24-28)*

Here we have two more unexceptionable evidences, that all things that were created by Christ, shall be made subject unto him, and indeed so subject, that all things will be put under him in that true order in which God in the beginning created them; for this is the import of the original word *upetaxen.*

But that is by no means the order of the creatures to live in sin, which is altogether *ataxia*, or disorder, and consequently to lie under the wrath of God, and in the fiery lake, or second death. In short, it is to be such a subjection, wherewith death (as is expressly added) that is, all that may be called by that name, and therefore not only the first, but in particular the second death, or fiery lake, and consequently sin as the sting of death will be entirely abolished, destroyed, and swallowed up in victory;[287] such a subjection as will be that of Christ's humanity, with his saints under God, yea, such a subjection, according to which, God, who is to be all in all in all things, may be all too in those creatures that before had been enemies of Christ, and had been lying in the fiery lake; because the expression of God's being all in all in the creatures, necessarily implies a state of perfect happiness, and shows that the whole mass of the creatures being made subject unto God and Christ, will be thus pervaded by God's Spirit, and, as one might say, in a sort deified (or made

286 1 Cor. 15:24–28
287 1 Cor. 15:54–56

partaken of the divine nature). God with them, and they with God, in a manner will be but one spirit, as the Holy Scripture expressly saith of such as are joined unto the Lord, or are subject unto him in truth.[288] But this is impossible to be so long as the creatures remain in sin and death; for then they are forsaken of God, and separated from him, which will be the highest degree of punishment in hell. Now if it is true that all creatures, and consequently also the enemies of Christ that are cast into the fiery lake, will be brought into that state of subjection just now described, wherein God will be all in all, then it must also be true that sin and all pain following it, which is found in the creatures, and of course the fiery lake too, must at last be altogether annihilated, because, without such an annihilation God cannot be all in all. If anyone would object here, that the present forced subjection of the devils under Christ and his people, mentioned in Luke 10:17-20, is likewise expressed by the word *upotasseta*, or to be subordinate; and that from hence appears, that, according to the Holy Spirit's judgment, this is the right subjection of evil spirits and damned men, and that, consequently there is no occasion to interpret the places mentioned, of a different sort of subjection of the damned:[289] To this I answer, that we must make a distinction between the commenced and the accomplished or perfect subjection of the apostatized creatures. It is indeed in some measure already the right subjection or subordination of evil spirits and men, when they are in such a manner overcome by the power of the spirit of Christ and his believers, that they are obliged to begin outwardly to bow under them, and to show them a forced obedience. But it is false that this should be that perfect subjection which God requires of his creatures (among which even the fallen angels are indisputably to be reckoned) since it is only a commenced subjection, and will make way for

---

288 1 Cor. 6:17 compared with John 17:21–23; 1 John 4:16
289 Heb. 2:8; 1 Cor. 15:24–28

that finally perfect and accomplished subordination, which according to our savior's own words, is this, when the creatures worship God in spirit and in truth, and so are not subject to him in a forced and affected manner, but willingly and gladly: for such and no other worshipers and subjects God seeketh.[290] It is evident that Luke 10:17-20 speaks only of a commenced subjection, which makes that which is evil begin to bow a little under that which is good, though at the same time evil in itself continues to be evil; whereas Heb. 2:8 and particularly 1 Cor. 15:24–28 speaks not only of a merely begun, but consummate subjection or subordination of all creatures, and therefore also of the fallen angels and damned men, as I have shown above from the import of the phrase of God's being all in all in the creatures.

> *"God also hath highly exalted him (Christ) and given him a name which is above every name; that at (or in) the name of Jesus every knee should bow, of things in heaven and things in earth, and (N.B.) things under the earth: And that every tongue should confess that Jesus Christ is Lord, to the glory of God the Father."[291] (Phil. 2:9-11)*

> *"And every creature which is in heaven, and on the earth, and (N.B.) under the earth, and such as are in the sea, and all that are in them, heard I, saying, Blessing, and honor, and glory and power, be unto him that sitteth upon the throne, and unto the Lamb, for ever and ever."[292] (Rev. 5:13)*

> *"All thy works shall praise thee, O Jehovah, and thy*

---

290 John 4:23-24 compared with Matt. 4:10
291 Phil. 2:9-11
292 Rev. 5:13

saints shall bless thee."[293] *(Psalm 145:10)*

"Let every thing that hath breath praise Jah;"[294]
(Psalm 150:6)

Hallelujah! These sentences again afford us a fine explanation of the before described general subjection of all creatures, according to which every creature, or work of God, and consequently also Lucifer with his angels, shall acknowledge Christ for their Lord, and bless God, and praise him, which cannot be as long as the creatures are in a state of condemnation, wicked, and enemies of God.

"For this purpose the Son of God was manifested, that
he might destroy the works of the devil."[295] *(1 John 3:8)*

Whatsoever, therefore, is a work of the devil, and belongs to the serpent's head, or to that government established by him through self-will, in opposition to the kingdom of God, must be destroyed by the Son of God: for that is his office. Now sin in all creatures, as well in Lucifer himself and his angels, as in man seduced by him, is not a work of God, but of the devil (and belongs to the hellish serpent's head) which Lucifer, by the turning away of his will from God, and thus becoming a devil, has first brought into himself, and the rest of the rebellious angels, and afterward also into man: Therefore must Christ at last annihilate and utterly destroy sin, together with death, and all unhappiness as its reward, in all creatures, as well apostate angels as fallen men. For if he was not to do this in all fallen creatures, he would not destroy all the works of the devil, but leave many satanical works undestroyed, and consequently he would not completely

---

293 Psalm 145:10
294 Psalm 150:6. Or properly, "Every thing that hath breath shall praise Jah."
295 1 John 3:8

execute his office; but be it far from us to think thus of him. For Christ must, as was said before, bruise the serpent's head;[296] and in an unlimited manner abolish or undo sin, for which purpose he made a sacrifice of himself, according to Heb. 9:26. After which bruising of the serpent's head, and abolishing of sin, no other but altogether holy angels and righteous men will remain, in whom God may be all in all.

> "And he that sat upon the throne, said, Behold, I make all things new. And he said unto me: Write, for these words are true and faithful."[297] (Rev. 21:5)

This promise is adapted to what we read;[298] and shows again that we have no right to exclude one individual creature of all those that are fallen into sin and lie under the curse, from the renovation and final restoration, because the promise absolutely declares that all things shall be made new.

> "And he (Jesus) said unto them (his disciples) Go ye into all the world, and preach the gospel to every creature."[299] (Mark 16:15)

That is, go ye forth into all the world, and proclaim, wherever ye go, the glad tidings that such a savior is come, who both can, and really will, in that order of repentance and faith appointed by God for that purpose, take away all sin, and all wretchedness hanging together with it, from all creatures laboring under the same. And that the apostles preached no other Gospel but this, which concerneth all creatures, Paul declares in plain terms:

> "If ye continue in the faith, grounded and settled, and be not moved away from the hope of the Gospel,

296 Gen. 3:15
297 Rev. 21:5
298 Gen 1:31
299 Mark 16:15

> which ye have heard, and which was preached (or, is
> preaching) to every creature under heaven."[300] (Col.
> 1:23)

Now by what has been said, let all pious Christians, nay, all reasonable men in the world, judge who they are that in the plainest and simplest manner, without false glosses of blind and carnal reasoning, understand the above cited clear testimonies; whether those who hope from them for a general restoration of all things; or those who in a rash manner exclude from the pitying love of God, the universal reconciliation of Christ, and the final renovation (which in the said texts are extended in an unlimited manner, over God's whole creation), many thousands of millions of rational creatures.

Of all the places brought from the Holy Scriptures against the restoration of fallen angels, that which we find in Heb. 2:16 is reckoned none of the least considerable, which in the common English translation runs thus:

> "For verily he (Christ) took not on him the nature of
> angels; but he took on him the seed of Abraham."[301]
> (Heb. 2:16)

From which words the inference is drawn, that since Christ has not taken on him the nature of angels, he consequently cannot have redeemed and reconciled those of them that did not keep their principalities, but rebelled against their Maker, incurring thereby his indignation; and that therefore, they being not redeemed nor reconciled by Christ, can never be restored by him. But let me have never so much regard for the translators of the Bible, yet I must own that the rendering of these words in the aforesaid manner, does not at all express the meaning of the

---

300 Col. 1:23
301 Heb. 2:16

original; which better agrees with the following marginal reading of most large Bibles: "For verily, he (Christ) taketh not hold
of angels, but of the seed of Abraham he taketh hold." Now,
Christ's not taking hold of angels, does no more signify his not
taking the nature of angels on him, than his taking hold of the
seed of Abraham signifies his taking human nature upon him.
But when it is said of Christ in this place, that he taketh hold of
the seed of Abraham, it naturally means, that he chooseth, ap-
propriateth unto himself, and regardeth as his own and his peculiar people, the spiritual seed of Abraham,[302] that is, all believers
from among the Jews and Gentiles, and that he taketh hold of
them as something extraordinary and very precious; that he does
not only hold them fast himself, but has also recommended them
to the particular care of his heavenly Father, out of whose hands
none is able to pluck them.[303] Yea, that he taketh hold of them by
receiving them into his most intimate communion and fellow-
ship, even his spiritual consanguinity, and taking them for his
brethren, according to the foregoing eleventh, and twelfth verses,
and following seventeenth verse; in making them joint heirs
with him, partakers of his glory, kings and priests in the world
or age to come, which God hath not put in subjection unto angels, as we read Heb. 2:5, but unto his Son, and his first born
brethren, who are also called God's elect and the bride of Christ.
In short, Christ taking hold of the seed of Abraham, proves the
prerogative of the faithful above all creatures both in heaven and
in earth.

And what is further the purport of the words, he taketh not
hold of angels? This we may easily conceive from what has been
said. It is not, as I have already observed, that Christ did not take
upon him an angelical nature; but it means briefly, that Christ
has not chosen the angels for such high degrees of glory as those

302 Gal. 3:29
303 John 10:29

who among men believe in him; that they are not of Christ's brethren, nor are we to have a share in the government and priesthood of the world to come, being only ministers for the heirs of salvation.

Another very strong argument, that this is the most natural and unconstrained sense of the above cited text of Scripture, is because we do not find so much as one place in the whole Bible, whereby the seed of Abraham is understood the human nature, or whole race of men in general. And why should angels here intend the nature of the angels considered in itself? What has been said, I think, is sufficient to show evidently, that it is not possible that from the text in question, there can be the least objection raised against the fallen angels being at last restored by Christ. And I am of opinion, that on the contrary, there is rather hid in it a proof for their final restoration. For to that exceeding great and more than angelical glory of Christ's elect in the next world, or age, belongs indisputably too, that they shall judge angels;[304] which words divines commonly understand of the judgments and punishments unto which the elect will help to condemn the evil spirits, and which is the true sense of that place, but whether it be the entire sense of it, is another question. Now the aim of all punishments in the world or age to come, unto which Christ and his bride will sentence all creatures that have rebelled against him, is this, that they may humble themselves before him, and thus be put in a condition, that at last through the power of his blood, shed for the whole world, and consequently for all creatures in which sin is found, they may be cleansed therefrom, and the diabolical image destroyed, and so may be made subject unto God in truth. Yea, as sure God is God, that is essentially and invariably Love towards all his creatures, and is to be such to all endless eternity, so sure it is, that all his judg-

---

304 1 Cor. 6:3

ments can have no other aim but that which was just now mentioned; let people say what they will against it.

And when this scope of the divine judgment upon the fallen angels (after the example of the proud, but afterward humbled king of Babylon)[305], shall be obtained, as certainly one day or other it must, according to the plain testimony of the word of God, which says that even all things under the earth (viz. damned angels and men, as all divines understand it) shall bow their knees before Jesus Christ, and confess that he is Lord, to the glory of God the Father:[306] When, I say, this shall be accomplished, then the fallen angels will be no longer proud devils, but humbled spirits, and truly in such a condition, that God by the Son of his eternal love (by whom both the visible and invisible things were created)[307] can save them from perdition. For God's maxim, which necessarily flows from his being, is once for all, that God resisteth the proud creatures only, and giveth grace to the humble,[308] and indeed without respect of persons,[309] be they now called men or angels.

He loves one creature as well as another; although he makes of the one a more glorious vessel than of the other. In this he cannot be hindered neither by the multitude nor heinousness of the sins before committed by the creatures. For, where sin aboundeth, grace and love shall much more abound, viz. then when the creature has acknowledged its sin and by the powerful grace of God leaves off sinning. In fine, that will be done, which is spoken in Rev. 21:5. God will make all things, that are old and spoiled, new again.

"These words are true and faithful." Amen.

---

305 Dan. 4:31–34 compared with Isa. 14:4
306 Phil. 2:10-11
307 Col. 1:16
308 1 Pet. 5:5
309 Rom. 2:11; Col 3:25

XIII.

INQUIRY, WHETHER THIS SACRED TRUTH MAY MAKE MEN CARELESS? OF THE EXCELLENT USEFULNESS OF IT: AND WHAT IS TO BE THOUGHT OF THE CONTRARY DOCTRINE.

THE right comprehension of this holy truth of the Restoration of all Things, cannot make one single man careless, or give him the least occasion or license to sin. For, how can such a doctrine make one careless, which teacheth that the wrath of God abideth on a man as long as he continueth in sin; and that in proportion to the growth and increase of sin in man, so for his torment, the anger of God increases more and more incessantly; insomuch that this tormenting fire cannot be quenched before its com-bustible, namely sin, is destroyed? which point is the very heart and marrow of this doctrine. If one was to teach, that God would not punish men for their sins in the next world, such doctrine would tend to make them careless. But that cannot be said of us, who believe and maintain the blessed doctrine of the restoration of all things in a scriptural manner, and teach with our beloved Lord Jesus, the universal savior and Reconciler of the world, that a man must give an account for every idle word in the day of judgment, unless he repents of it in this life; and consequently, much more for all other and greater sins; and shall not only suf-fer a certain and most painful punishment for them all in the next world, but also, by the neglecting of this present time of grace, he will deprive himself of the enjoyment of an unspeak-able glory; viz. of the heavenly birth-right, or the joint govern-ment with Christ in the world to come, and the celestial priesthood, for ever and ever, so that he will never be able to obtain it again, if even he was to seek carefully with the bitterest tears of repentance to recover it.[310] Yea, if all the holy angels and elect of God were to make intercession for him in this respect, it would be to no purpose.[311]

But by believing and teaching that all corrupt creatures shall be made good again, and all that is called sin, death, devil, and hell, shall be annihilated or entirely destroyed, we no more make men careless, than Christ and his apostles made men careless, who taught and commanded to teach the same;[312] as has been shown sufficiently in the preceding chapter from many plain testimonies of God's word.

If the terrible judgments of the next world, wherewith God threatens all obdurate sinners, were only to last as long as this life-time, it would be a motive more than sufficient to keep all discreet and prudent people from all carnal security. For what discreet person, who has but a little honesty left, would choose to commit for twenty, thirty, forty, or fifty years all imaginable wickedness, if he certainly knew that he was at last to die an ignominious death for it, that he was to be hanged, broke on the wheel, or burnt alive? Now, can the fear of such a short punishment, the lasting whereof is altogether disproportionate to the lasting of the sin, in a discreet person overcome or entirely check the inclination to sin? How much more then ought it to restrain a man from sin, when we teach according to truth, that if he does not repent from his heart of all his transgressions in this time of grace, and earnestly follow Christ in self-denial, and regeneration, he will in the world to come, not only be excluded to all endless eternity from all the inexpressible glories annexed to the spiritual birth-right, but that moreover he will be obliged to

---

310 Heb. 12:16-17 compared with Gen. 27:34–38; Prov. 1:24–31; Luke 14:24
311 1 John 5:16
312 Mark 16:15 compared with Col. 1:23; Gal. 1:8-9

remain daring a terrible long periodical eternity, or perhaps during all those ages of the next world, that is, many thousands of years; in the most horrid and intolerable pain; though at last being humbled in a dreadful manner, he may and will, through the endless mercy of God, obtain some portion of grace after all.

But whose hearts can endure, or whose hands can be strong, in the time that God shall deal thus with them for their sins? Who can bear the thought of enduring such a long and dreadful punishment, for a short life of sin? The sinners of the old world that perished by the deluge, afford us an undeniable instance of the amazing length of future misery; they were shut up in the woeful prison of the first death; almost two thousand and four hundred years, in darkness, misery, and despair, before the Gospel of the grace of God was preached to them by Christ.[313] Ah! do but think what they must have suffered during all that terrible long period! I dare say that it made them lose all their appetite for sin.

Now, since the pains of the first death are so terrible and lasting, how dreadful beyond conception, and of what long continuance must the intolerable pains of the second death be! that lake of fire and brimstone! O how it will torment such who turn the grace of God into lasciviousness, and make the clear light of the Gospel (which did not shine so bright to sinners of old as it does to us) subservient to their carnal carelessness, and to fortify themselves thereby in their works of darkness, and in all manner of iniquity![314]

But whosoever is of the opinion, that, in order to preserve people from all carelessness, it is necessary to threaten them with such painful punishments as are absolutely endless, and to last as long as God exists, such a one thinks wrong: for that would not be the truth, and the untruth is not a proper mean for

313 1 Pet. 3:19; 1 Pet. 4:6
314 See Heb. 10:26–31; Jude 4; 2 Pet. 2:1–3; Rev. 21:8

the conversion and salvation of men.

God sanctifieth us only through his truth.[315] If absolutely end-less punishments had been true, Christ would certainly have held them forth plainly to impenitent sinners: but we do not find that he has done so. With eternal or *aionion* punishments indeed he has threatened them; but what is to be understood by that word has been mentioned before, and is best explained by him-self, saying:

> *"Verily, I say unto thee, thou shalt by no means come out thence (namely out of the prison), till thou hast paid the uttermost farthing."*[316] *(Matt. 5:26)*

> *"And that servant who knew his Lord's will, and prepared not himself, nor did according to his will, shall be beaten with many stripes. But he that knew not, and did commit things worthy of stripes, shall be beaten with few stripes," etc.*[317] *(Luke 12:47-48)*

Now, this cannot mean as long as God shall exist, but shows incontestably, a certain term or end of the confinement in the in-fernal prison; which end will be upon the complete suffering of all well deserved punishments for every sin, of which men do not repent in this time of grace, even idle words and bad thoughts not excepted.[318]

Therefore, it remains true that this holy doctrine of the final Restoration of all Things, is rather the most effectual remedy against all carelessness; and whosoever looks rightly into this truth, will be most powerfully incited thereby to repentance and sanctification.

315 John 17:17
316 Matt. 5:26; Luke 12:58-59
317 Luke 12:47-48
318 Matt. 12:36; Matt. 15:19; 1. Cor. 4:5; Heb. 4:12

For, in the first place, it demonstrates the absolute necessity of sanctification with the greatest emphasis.

Secondly, it shows the unutterably great preeminence in glory, which those who suffer themselves to be sanctified and cleansed from all sin in their life-time here, will enjoy in the next state above all the rest, who in this time have neglected their sanctification.

Thirdly, it opens most perfectly the sole source and spring of all power to attain unto true sanctification, by representing according to its breadth, length, depth, and height, the boundless love of God in Christ Jesus; and showing the everlasting, universal, and eternally efficacious merits of our savior, and his immense fulness, from which we derive all power for the mortifying of our sins, and becoming truly godly. And, consequently, this enlivening knowledge of the infinite love of Christ tends to fill us with all the fulness of God.[319]

Fourthly, it banishes from the heart all servile or painful fear, which very much hinders a man's progress in Christianity,[320] and instead of it, brings a filial fear and love into the soul. For who would not love and adore such a God, whose love towards all his creatures is so immensely great, that he cannot rest, as one may say, till he has recovered all that was lost, and drawn it into the communion of his beatitude! And who would not at the same time in a child-like manner fear that God, who, indeed, on the one hand, is gracious to such as love him, but also, on the other hand, punishes, without respect of persons, all such as sin, and continues his judgments so long, as till the proud and obstinate creature humbles itself before him, approving of the punishment of its transgressions, and suffering the most holy justice of God, as a sharp two-edged sword, to cut off from it the very being and root of sin, in a severe but necessary process! Now, I cannot con-

319 Eph. 3:18-19
320 Rom. 8:15; 2 Tim. 1:7; 1 John 4:18

ceive, how, on the contrary, that doctrine can bring forth such good fruits, according to which we represent to ourselves God (who is universal and eternal love) as merely endless fury towards most of his creatures, that is, as no God at all.

Fifthly, it shows us the exceeding great and almighty power of our savior Jesus Christ, and thereby exceedingly encourages us in our combat against sin. For, if Christ be really such a savior, who both can and will actually at last eradicate sin and death out of all creatures; why should not this Almighty savior be also able to sanctify us through and through, and to deliver at now from all unrighteousness? In the meanwhile we may allow, that as every thing which is good, even so this holy truth may be abused and misapplied by the wicked to their own ruin and destruction.[321] But this cannot prejudice the truth itself, nor make that to be false which is true. Nay, it will rather serve to make the wicked stand the more inexcusable in the day of judgment, and vindicate the divine justice in condemning them for not repenting, though the whole counsel of God was revealed to them. Do not most of those that are called protestant Christians, to this day, make a wrong use of the sacred gospel doctrines, and of the faith set forth thereby? But what protestant minister will allow that the doctrine of the protestants is hurtful, because it is misapplied? This holy truth of the restoration of all things delivers all who receive it in the love of it, from all their hard thoughts of God, and from all their anxious scruples about the universal love, mercy, holiness, justice, wisdom, omnipotence, and truth of God, because it represents all the divine attributes in the finest harmony. For, according to this doctrine, how can any person have the least doubt of God's earnest love and mercy towards all men, yea, towards all his creatures in general, that want to be pitied by him, when he hears, that God is not only willing to deliver all

---

321 2 Cor. 2:15-16; Jude 4; Rom. 2:4–6; Rom. 3:5–8; Tit. 1:15-16

from their misery, but that at last he also will deliver every one without exception, and grant them all really to enjoy his tender mercies? Do you not think that there is a sufficient inference to be drawn from this doctrine what a holy Being that God must be who can have no communication with anything that is unholy, and cannot suffer the corrupt creatures to come before his face, till they are most perfectly cleansed from all their sins, so that neither spot or wrinkle thereof can be any more discerned upon them? Ah! how ought men to use all earnest endeavors to be sanctified by times, in order to be soon received into the communion of this holy God, and not be so long banished from him! And whosoever farther considers, with what unspeakably great glory this God rewards all such as make good use of this present time of grace, and how severely he punishes all impenitent sinners and hypocrites for all their sins, not the least excepted, both by the first and second death, and indeed in such a manner, that in proportion to and according to the nature of the sin, both in severity and duration of the punishment are exactly ordered,[322] and at last will serve to humble the wicked creatures to the utmost before their Creator, and to dispose them to suffer sin to be entirely separated from them. Whosoever, I say, considers this, will own with me, that this God is a most just Being, who loves righteousness. And must he not be infinitely wise who knows how to bring all his divine counsels to pass without suffering any part of his plan to fail? And must not this God also be Almighty, who can in such a manner cast down to the ground all creatures that oppose him, let them be never so strong and numerous, so that at last they must give up the victory, and with all their heart become subject to him? And lastly, if you will also be certain how true the Holy Scriptures are, which contain the uttered and written words of God, and how all things therein fore-

322 As Christ teaches us in Luke 12:47-48; Matt. 11:22-24; Luke 10:12-14

told shall be entirely accomplished, do but consider the holy doctrine of the restoration of all things, and you will see how it is nothing else but a most exact and perfect fulfilling of the Scriptures, and of every thing that God has manifested therein, concerning his love, mercy, holiness, justice, wisdom, power, etc.

By means of this holy doctrine likewise many points in controversy among the different sects in Christendom may be determined and decided, and consequently a good foundation laid for the uniting the Christian world, which at present is divided into so many parties. For instance, this holy truth most plainly shows what God's punishing justice is, namely, not a tyrannical revengefulness, having for its aim nothing else but the pain and misery of the creatures; but such a holy attribute of the supreme God, which is grounded in his eternal love, and by virtue whereof he must indeed at last let the disobedient creatures, that will not be ruled by his Spirit, forcibly feel what they choose, or punish them both in this and the next world according to equity, as long as they continue in their wickedness; however so, that not the pain itself, which the creatures feel through their own fault, much less an endless duration of such pain, but an eternal destruction of sin, and the entire separation of it from the creatures, is the ultimate end of their punishment, which also at last must be actually obtained.

O how venerable does this right idea of God's punishing justice make it to an enlightened soul! How gladly does the soul bow under it in this time of grace, suffering this holy justice to mortify all that is evil, and to sever it from the soul, though the operation be painful, so that it may not experience the severity of this holy justice in the next world, when the fire of the divine wrath will be all in a blaze.

This holy doctrine likewise shows the right foundation of divine election and eternal reprobation, and demonstrates both to

Lutherans and Calvinists as well wherein each party is right, as what they want of the full understanding of this important point.

The doctrine of the Lutherans is orthodox, which teaches that God with great earnest will have all men saved, and that he also really saves those who during this time of grace come to believe in Christ, and persevere in faith, and that from eternity he has predestined them for eternal life. But it is without foundation, that therefore they want to exclude to all endless eternity, from all participation of the divine mercy, the rest in general that do not believe to this elect; and this is owing to their not discerning the great difference between the prerogative of the heavenly birth-right, to which is annexed an exceeding great glory, and the common portion in the blessed subjection in the kingdom of God. So also what the Calvinists teach, that those shall be actually saved, whom God will have to be saved, is indeed a scriptural truth: But the additional conclusion is good for nothing, that since but a few men are saved, consequently God will have but the least number saved. Or, although he does in some sort desire the salvation of all men (as some among them own) yet, say they, he will not really give faith to all men, which in reality is the same with the former. But the holy doctrine of the restoration of all things, shows them, that at last all men will actually be made subject unto God, and consequently, every one in his degree, be made happy. Therefore, they must indeed in good earnest hold fast the before-mentioned truth, but amend the rest of their doctrine in the following manner, and make this conclusion: Those whom God will have to be saved, will actually be saved. Now God plainly declares in his word, that he will have all men to be saved; therefore all men will be really saved at last; though indeed in such a manner, that only the elect, or firstborn, will enjoy the prerogative of the birthright, or the joint government with Christ in the world to come, and the rest of men be forced to undergo the judgment of the first death, and perhaps of the second death also, and at last, when they are purged from their sins, be obliged to take up with but a common portion of happiness.

This sacred doctrine is further capable to decide the dispute between us and the Roman Catholics about Purgatory: For it shows the truth of the purification of souls after their departure out of this world, without the least prejudice to the doctrine of Christ's merits or any other important article of faith. The truth of the purification of souls in the next world, as far as it is grounded in the Holy Scripture, we must necessarily grant to the Roman Catholics, if we would convince them of the rest of their errors respecting purgatory; for this we shall never be able to do as long as we deny what the Scriptures affirm concerning it.

The contrary doctrine, which is diametrically opposite to the blessed restoration of all things, teaches: That but the smallest number, and perhaps not a thousandth part of the fallen creatures, will be really brought again to God, by the universal redemption of Christ; and that the greatest part by far, must remain in everlasting misery so long as God exists. But far be it from me to impute this doctrine to all protestants in general; for I am persuaded, that, on the contrary, there are many among them, who either entirely approve of the blessed doctrine of the restoration; or if for the present they have not a perfect knowledge of it, yet understand some truths leading to it, and do not dispeople the glorious kingdom of Christ in such a manner as is done by the doctrine just now mentioned. But, however, the number of those being but too great, who with all the faculties of their souls stick close to the said doctrine, and in an unjustifiable manner cry down the holy doctrine of the blessed restoration as a dangerous heresy, condemned long ago, though it manifestly exalts the majesty of God in every respect, and aims at the entire destruction of the empire of sin; I cannot help, before I come to a conclusion, admonishing and desiring them in a few words, to take care that their own doctrine be not such as they undeservedly describe ours to be, and not to be too rash in judging and condemning other servants of Christ with their doctrine, which they neither understand nor will understand, and which is so far from teaching anything that is bad, that it speaks of nothing but what is good. I ask them upon their conscience, whether their above mentioned doctrine, according to which, God and Christ are to have but the smallest number of souls for their share, the most being obliged to remain to all eternity in the empire and under the power of the devil; I ask them, I say, whether this doctrine does not make sin and darkness stronger and more powerful than God, the redemption of Christ, and the Light, I dare say, they will not own it, but it is so in reality, as has been shown in different places of this treatise. They think, indeed, that men can be most effectually roused from the slumber of their carnal security, and incited to repentance, by confining the real extent of God's mercy only to this short lifetime, and making it of none effect, and depriving all corrupt creatures of it after their decease, to all endless eternity. But they only imagine and think so; and the effects of their good intention are but indifferent. For as this doctrine gives people a notion that immediately after death either a full endless damnation, or the perfect joys of heaven are to begin; it makes them think that if they do but find some good motions within themselves, not leading a vicious life, they must be sufficiently converted, so that it would be impossible for God in the condition they are in to let them be damned forever, but that immediately after their decease he must necessarily receive them into heaven. Therefore, they remain indolent in the exercise of their Christian duties, and their highest degree of perfection is but a Pharisaical honesty; but they know nothing of an earnest diligence in sanctification, or a cleansing of themselves from all filthiness of flesh and spirit. And all this is generally occasioned by such teachers who are mortal enemies of the blessed restoration, and who at the same time condemn and persecute true Christianity and piety.

Now, as the doctrine of endless damnation and torment is no true motive for sanctification, so it is likewise void of all comfort; for if a man's conscience begins to waken, especially at the end of his life, when the devil uses all his power to bring a soul to the utmost despair, and it begins to see that it is not only as bad as the most wicked of men, but as the devil himself, nay, worse, on account of its having so long resisted God in his working out of its salvation; and that therefore it cannot be saved, except the devil himself was to be saved (and that really there is in some measure a more than diabolical iniquity in man, has been shown in another place of this treatise; for which reason also some men, viz. the Beast and False Prophet, will be cast into the fiery lake a thousand years sooner than the devil himself)[323]. What can the enemies of the Restoration say to such a soul at that time! will their doctrine be able to save it from despair? I say, no. Is it not the blessed doctrine of the Restoration which alone is able to comfort the poor creature, by representing in the most lively manner the everlastingness of God's mercy, and praising most gloriously the infinite power of the merits of Christ, as far surpassing all the might of sin; showing plainly at the same time the proper end of all God's judgments both in this and the next world to be no other than the destruction of sin and the final and general well-being of all creatures, and by declaring most comfortably, what a great advantage it will be to the souls to submit here in this time under God's holy justice, and to suffer themselves here to be condemned and judged according to their

---

323 According to Rev. 19:20 compared with Rev. 20:10

deserts, but then at once to sink down into the abyss of the ever-lasting mercy of God, and the ever-efficacious merits of Christ? All which is impossible to be effected by the common doctrine of the partial mercy of God, limited only within the time of this world, which doctrine also represents the punishing justice of God as having also for its ultimate end the everlasting pain of the wicked creatures.

Lastly, let me ask, whether the doctrine opposite to that of the blessed Restoration, does not give occasion to atheistic minds to make that cursed mockery which they do of the Scriptures, even to the denying of the being of God? Since indeed, on the one hand this doctrine speaks of a great many glorious things in God; of his love, mercy, grace, omnipotence, truth, etc., but on the other hand, mixes such dogmas therewith, which in a great measure contradict all the former good and glorious things that were spoken in praise of the Godhead, and represent God, conse-quently, under such a character as it is impossible that any rea-sonable man should conceive as becoming the Deity, and which may easily make men fall entirely into atheism. For instance, it praises in God, first, that he has made many glorious promises in his word, and that he is to perform great matters; for example, that he will make all things new again that have been spoiled; that he is willing to convert all men to himself, and to save them, as also, that he will destroy the whole kingdom of the devil, etc. But at last all the great things that God is to do, mean nothing else, according to this doctrine, than that God indeed has promised to do all this, but that in reality only the least part of it shall be fulfilled.

Secondly, the doctrine of endless damnation makes also many fine words of God's compassionate heart, and of his universal love and mercy; but if one comes to examine the affair closely, it amounts to this, that in reality God is not so merciful and compassionate at a sinful man. For instance, David, who was a man as we are, had so much compassion for his son Absalom, that he wished to have died for him, because Absalom died in his sins, and did not go to a very good place;[324] but of our God, who is love and mercy essentially, people would have us believe that with the hour of death all his mercy for a man has ceased to all endless eternity. But Jesus Christ himself, the eternal truth, and not our own reason, has taught us to make a quite different conclusion.[325] Which also follows from what the great God also says of himself.[326]

Thirdly, the before-mentioned doctrine does likewise speak in praise of God, that indeed he hates nothing in his creatures but only what is evil, namely, sin; but that he very much loves the creature itself, or that which is good. Wherefore it is said, that, *Diabolus entitative bonus*, or the devil himself according to his being, is good, and so far as he is the creature of God is not excluded from his love. But then, if it is true, what this doctrine adds, that God by punishing his wicked creatures has not for his ultimate end and aim the recovery and restoration, but the endless torment of the creature, then no natural man, who is acute, can possibly make any other conclusion, than that God does not only abhor evil, but even that which is good, namely, the creature, or the works of his hands. And is it not an easy matter for such a man, when he hears so many contradictory positions, which are altogether given out for true and salutary words of God, to fall away so far as to believe nothing at all for the future of the truth of Scripture? But eternal glory be to the Most High, for having given us to know and to taste with great certainty, from his word, by the revelation of his good Spirit, his majestic, most holy, and alone adorable Being of Love, out of whom,

---

324 2 Sam. 18:30; 2 Sam. 19:4
325 Matt. 7:11; Luke 11:13
326 Jonah 4:10-11

through whom, and into whom are all things. By this knowledge, we may be most powerfully preserved from all wickedness and atheism of these latter abominable times. Yea, honor, glory, and praise be to him for ever and ever.

Amen!

Hallelujah!

THE END

INDEX OF BIBLICAL REFERENCES

INDEX OF BIBLICAL REFERENCES

Made in the USA
Coppell, TX
13 November 2023

24173091R00092